FRONTIER FAKE NEWS

FRONTIER FAKE NEWS

*Nevada's Sagebrush
Humorists and Hoaxsters*

RICHARD MORENO

UNIVERSITY OF NEVADA PRESS | *Reno & Las Vegas*

University of Nevada Press | Reno, Nevada 89557 USA
www.unpress.nevada.edu
Copyright © 2023 by University of Nevada Press
All rights reserved
Manufactured in the United States of America

FIRST PRINTING

Cover photographs courtesy of the Library of Congress; Special Collections and University Archives Department, University of Nevada, Reno; and DTParker1000.

LIBRARY OF CONGRESS CATALOGING-IN-PUBLICATION DATA
Names: Moreno, Richard, author.
Title: Frontier fake news : Nevada's sagebrush humorists and hoaxsters / Richard Moreno.
Description: Reno : University of Nevada Press, [2022] | Includes bibliographical references and index. | Summary: "*Frontier Fake News: Nevada's Sagebrush Humorists and Hoaxsters* explores some of the earliest perpetrators of fake news. Legendary Nevada writers like Mark Twain, Dan De Quille, Sam Davis, and others were renowned for their clever and mischievous hoaxes, satires, puns, and other witticisms designed to entertain their readers while often making a political statement."—Provided by publisher.
Identifiers: LCCN 2022038188 | ISBN 9781647790868 (paperback) | ISBN 9781647790875 (ebook)
Subjects: LCSH: Twain, Mark, 1835–1910—Friends and associates. | Journalists—Nevada—History—19th century. | Wit and humor in journalism—Nevada—History—19th century. | Fake news—Nevada—History—19th century. | Satirists—History—19th century. | Frontier and pioneer life—Nevada—19th century. | Nevada—History—19th century.
Classification: LCC F841 .M586 2022 | DDC 979.3/01—dc23/eng/20220823
LC record available at https://lccn.loc.gov/2022038188

I dedicate this book to my amazing parents,

Richard and Maureen Moreno, who passed away in 2020.

They always encouraged me to follow my own path

and were there whenever I needed them.

I miss them both so much.

Contents

Illustrations follow page 90.

Acknowledgments

THIS WORK RECOGNIZES and applauds the pioneering scholars, historians, and writers who brought to light the brilliance of a pack of nineteenth-century Nevada journalists. These frontier newspapermen showed the courage to speak truth to power, often through humor and satire. The men and women who subsequently focused on these western journalists rightly sought to ensure that they will never be forgotten, and I now enthusiastically join them in that mission.

I offer my thanks and most sincere appreciation to the University of Nevada Press publisher, JoAnne Banducci, and to my editors, Margaret Dalrymple, Curtis Vickers, and Kathleen Chapman. I would also like to thank Lawrence Berkove, Cheryl Glotfelty, Duncan Emrich, Ella Sterling Cummins, David W. Toll, Ronald M. and Susan James, and Richard Lingenfelter for rediscovering these journalistic giants, who crafted fake news for a purpose and who would have found plenty of material for their "quaints" if they were still around today.

Additionally, I want to offer thanks to my good friend Martin Griffith for his welcome advice; to the previously mentioned Ron James for his insights and astute observations, which truly helped improve this book; to Ed Komenda for his last-minute help with my research; and to my wife, Pam, for her patience as I too often regaled her with old-time newspaper stories and facts.

FRONTIER FAKE NEWS

Introduction

In on the Joke

I HAVE A CONFESSION. In the mid-1980s, shortly after I had traded in my press card for a press kit, I read a copy of the revived *Territorial Enterprise and Virginia City News*, the famous former home of Mark Twain and Dan De Quille, which stated that the Comstock-based newspaper wanted to resuscitate the rollicking spirit and traditions of its early days. I knew, of course, that Twain and others at the *Enterprise* were famous for their hoaxes—what today we would call genuine fake news. Plus, I really, really wanted to write an article in that same vein and to publish it in the legendary newspaper.

So, I wrote a fake press release. In it, I said that a mining company, which I called United Minerals Consolidated Ltd., had recently announced plans to purchase all of Virginia City, NV, in order to remove the entire community and dig the biggest open-pit mine in the state. I made up a fake president for my fake mining company, Winslow P. Patterson, and quoted him as saying that testing had indicated the presence of vast gold and silver resources beneath the town, which could only be recovered by relocating or removing the community.

I thought the story would seem somewhat plausible because a real mining company with a similar name—United Mining Corporation—had been actively working in the Comstock area for several years, and there had been some talk that they wanted to revive underground mining in the region, which might include reopening mining tunnels located beneath the city. In the same way that Twain sought to use his hoaxes to side-eye his personal and political targets, my goal was to use satire and exaggeration to make a statement about the fragile nature of Virginia City, a community that I have loved deeply for a long time.

In an attempt to make the proposal even more absurd, I wrote that Patterson had a ludicrous plan calling for United Minerals to set up a table on the corner of C and Union Streets in Virginia City, where the company would offer cash on the spot to anyone wishing to sell their property.

"Nevada mining law allows us to condemn and acquire any property we want," I quoted Patterson as saying. "We will pay market rates for all property but won't be afraid to condemn parcels owned by people reluctant to part with them."

The release noted that the table would be set up from 8 AM to 5 PM on Mondays, Wednesdays, and Fridays for two weeks in early November, and it asserted that any land not purchased during that stretch would be acquired using "legal condemnation proceedings." It also said that United Minerals was a Delaware-based mining company and that its plans included razing the downtown, converting the Fourth Ward School into mining company offices, and rebuilding the former Virginia & Truckee Railroad line to carry ore from the pit to a new Southern Pacific Railroad line being built to Carson City. The release concluded with a statement from Patterson saying that the company was also considering purchasing all of the adjacent community of Gold Hill in order to dig a second, giant, open-pit mine at a later date.

I recall typing up my fake news release, placing it a generic, white envelope with a fake address, and then driving to Reno to mail it, so that it would not be sent from Carson City, where I was living at the time. I sent it anonymously because, while I was kind of proud of my hoax, I wasn't sure if anyone else would find it as humorous as I did—and I didn't want to get fired from the state public relations job I had at the time.

A few weeks later, I picked up the October 18, 1985, edition of the *Enterprise* and spotted my little release, published on page 9. Naturally, I thought it was great, so I immediately typed up a follow-up, fake release. This time, I wrote that in response to local protests about United Minerals' plans for Virginia City, the mining company had compromised and decided to only purchase and raze half of the historic city. According to my invented president, Winslow P. Patterson, the mining company would buy "all of the property east of C Street. . . . The rest of the community will remain on the mountainside overlooking the pit." He said the mining company would build an eight-foot-high concrete wall along the east side of C Street to protect residents from the pit's mining operations. The release concluded by saying that once the open-pit mine is no longer productive, the mining company "plans to convert it into a country club and marina to be called 'Rancho Virginia.'"

As before, I mailed the news release anonymously to the paper and then waited to see if this one would be published too. I didn't have to wait long. The lead story on the front page of the December 13 issue carried the headline: "United Minerals Revises VC Open Pit Plan." Beneath the headline and above the story, which took up much of the front page, was a three-column-wide photo of some unnamed mining operation (I had not included a photo, so the paper had supplied its own).

Inside the issue, an editorial titled "Deny United Minerals" lifted the hoax to a whole new level. "United Minerals, a mining conglomerate hiding in the corporate wilds of Delaware, plans to raze downtown Virginia City, and so create the largest open pit eyesore ever attempted in Nevada," the editorial said indignantly. "As expected the hue and cry on the heels of this insane announcement has touched off a fire storm of protest all over the west."

Mustering its harshest criticism, the paper said, "Winslow P. Patterson, United Minerals' president, a balding, deceptively professional wimp in a three-piece, tweedy suit, says the nefarious scheme will be good for Nevada and the national economy. These undisguised scoundrels with their heinous plans for eminent domain would turn the heart of our community into a pile of slag and rubble. Can any reasonably intelligent citizen assume that these carpetbaggers are altruistic agents of a benevolent corporate giant bent on meeting America's mineral needs? Hah! Bah! Total hogwash!"

Then the *Enterprise*'s editor, Tom Grant (who wrote under the pen name M. Jidough), upped the ante by including his own take: "United Minerals has pulled this imperious grandstand scam before. In 1977, United Minerals discovered a major gold deposit under the town of Yellow Fork, MT. The company managed to bamboozle the gullible citizenry into selling out lock, stock, and barrel. In a few short months the town was a memory. . . . Let's not allow this heartless corporate giant to rape and pillage this community."

The same issue contained a letter to the editor decrying United Minerals' plans for Virginia City, allegedly from Bonnie S. Crain of San Mateo, CA, who described herself as a subscriber, a member of the National Trust for Historic Preservation, and the owner of forty acres in the Virginia Highlands area. Crane said that all of downtown Virginia City could be relocated to her property, and in return, she would give ninety-nine-year leases to all property owners. "I wish especially to see St. Mary's of the Mountains and the Presbyterian Church removed. Perhaps each diocese would finance it plus the upkeep and install a septic tank, and connect to electricity service. I can't afford it. The Territorial Enterprise Building could also continue publishing there in the same manner and under the same terms, as well as the Bucket of Blood and any other buildings."

Another letter, supposedly from Edmund C. Puddicombe of Joliet, IL, said, "I am plenty upset about the open-pit mine ruining everything between C Street and Sugar Loaf Mountain. It's just greed, not so much a patriotic move to save our country. There are plenty of other ore-bearing areas without ripping out, or defacing the entire Comstock."

A real letter from a representative of United Mining sought to clarify that *it* was not the same company as United Minerals. R. Trent McAuliffe, manager of lands and contracts for the company, wrote:

> I am writing to request a clarification in regard to two articles appearing in your October 18, 1985, and November 15, 1985, issues concerning United Minerals Consolidated Ltd. While we at United Mining Corporation can certainly appreciate satirical journalism, the publication of the two aforementioned articles is causing problems and interference with our business and personal relationships.
>
> United Mining Corporation has at all times attempted to foster good community relations, part of which is based upon trust and upon security of Virginia City's townspeople in knowing that United Mining was not interested in destroying the basic historic ambience of the Virginia City area of which mining is an integral part. . . . I have been contacted by irate shareholders demanding explanations for the insensitivity attributed to United Mining Corporation by virtue of your articles. I have been contacted by individual property owners, some of whom fear for their property, others of whom are wishing to sell off their property quickly.

This letter was followed by an editor's note that said, "We salute you! You guys are great sports and though we have had fun with the 'United Minerals' story, we agree that the time has come for us to give you the credit you deserve for your contributions to our community!"

On February 2, 1986, the *Los Angeles Times* printed an Associated Press story titled "Mark Twain Tradition: Newspaper's Sense of Humor Fails to Tickle Everyone," which said that the "hoaxes and wisecracks" of the owners of the new *Territorial Enterprise* were not being met with universal approval in Virginia City. "Ken Foose Sr., a local merchant serving on a newly formed Chamber of Commerce committee hoping to negotiate with

Jidough [editor Tom Grant], says one problem with the paper's hoaxes is that some people apparently believe them. Foose said he got a letter from a friend in Missouri who subscribes to the *Enterprise,* expressing his sorrow that the entire town was being torn down to make way for an open pit mine. Foose said the first time he saw the article he checked with a local mining company to see if the story was true."

And with that, I decided to follow Twain's lead: after one of his hoaxes got out of hand, he departed Virginia City, so I, too, "disappeared." I never sent another story to the *Enterprise,* which, perhaps not coincidentally, ceased publishing about two weeks later (it first unsuccessfully tried to become a magazine before completely folding), and I never spoke of my hoax to anyone.

But I bring it up now because what I sought to do in the 1980s with my pair of fake news releases was to echo the kind of fake news that was popu- lar in frontier Nevada. Between about 1862 and 1915, a number of Silver State newspapers, led by the *Territorial Enterprise,* indulged in tongue-in-cheek, concocted news and feature stories and also printed puns, clever witticisms, and other humorous items. Unlike the so-called fake news of contemporary times—which is usually legitimate news painted with that damning label because some politician doesn't agree with or like the actual facts—fake news of the frontier era was actually fake.

Oscar Lewis, who wrote several books about Nevada and the West in the mid-twentieth century, including a book about Austin titled *The Town That Died Laughing,* noted that the reason why Nevada's frontier journalists gravitated toward such humor was because of the challenging living condi- tions in the Silver State's mining camps and communities.

"Life in the early mining towns and camps of the west was, by and large, no bed of roses, for living conditions were primitive in the extreme, the work hard and its rewards problematical, and the facilities for recreation—save for the ever-present bars and gaming tables—conspicuous mainly by their absence," Lewis wrote in the book, based largely on the work of frontier- newspaper editor Fred H. Hart, who wrote for and edited Austin's *Reese River Reveille* from 1875 to 1878.

Perhaps because of such shortcomings, those who lived in these often- remote, isolated mining communities were, in Lewis's words, "a hearty and self-reliant lot," who would often improvise their own entertainments, including the telling of tall tales. He added, "The western frontiersman was catholic in his tastes, and he welcomed whatever might offer itself in the way of diversion—provided only that it afforded him an opportunity to laugh."

In this fertile environment, Nevada's frontier-satirizing scribes flourished. Lewis posited that the early newspaper editors recognized that providing actual news was probably secondary to entertaining the mining camp readers, hungry for something to—at least momentarily—take their minds off of the tedium and drudgery of their everyday existence.

"Thus, they filled their columns with all sorts of items designed to produce a chuckle; humorous anecdotes, hoaxes, satire, brief sketches poking good-natured fun at local events or customs, or holding up to none-too-mild ridicule the foibles of their fellow townsmen," Lewis wrote.

His observation echoes an earlier one made by Rollin M. Daggett, who was an editor at the *Territorial Enterprise* starting in the early 1860s. In 1893, on the occasion of the original demise of the *Enterprise* (which was subsequently revived several times), Daggett reminisced about the storied paper's satirists in a piece that he wrote for the *San Francisco Examiner,* saying that during his tenure, the two most gifted reporters at the newspaper were Mark Twain and Dan De Quille. "If news was a little scarce Mark Twain and Dan de Quille, with their fertile brains and active imaginations, could scare up a 'story' that would raise the old Harry [that is, "raise hell"]," he noted.

Twain scholar and historian Henry Nash Smith agreed with this assessment, writing in his 1957 book, *Mark Twain of the Enterprise,* "Nevada journalism of the 1860s was nonchalant and uninhibited, and a report of the most commonplace event was likely to veer into fantasy or humorous diatribe."

However, as Jack Highton, a longtime journalism professor at the University of Nevada, Reno, pointed out, Nevada's frontier reporters and editors did not invent the fake news story. In his 1990 book, *Nevada Newspaper Days: A History of Journalism in the Silver State,* Highton explained that earlier, made-up news accounts first appeared in eastern newspapers, including *The Sun* in New York, which had published a famous series of articles in 1835 alleging that an alien civilization had been discovered on the moon. But Highton echoed Lewis in noting that the motivation for such hoaxes "was humor and satire," especially if it served to divert readers from more-depressing, actual news.

Perhaps the most candid assessment of the Nevada fake-news phenomenon came from nineteenth-century editor Fred Hart, who concocted an entire fake social organization, the Sazerac Lying Club, and who published accounts of its fake meetings for several years, using real names, in the *Reese River Reveille* during his time at the newspaper. A compilation of Hart's writings, *The Sazerac Lying Club: A Nevada Book,* which he published in 1878, included an introduction in which he explained, "Lying, like other arts and sciences, keeps pace with our education, refinement, and culture, and is fast becoming familiarized to the American people. Though I have classed it with the arts and sciences, and although there is something artistic in the construction of a good lie, and notwithstanding that a good, square lie is a scientific triumph, still, I am of the opinion that lying should more properly be considered as an accomplishment."

He continued, "Today, to lie, and lie well, is meritorious, and besides there's money in it, which of itself is sufficient to make it commendable." However, he added that unlike the lies of politicians, stockbrokers, newspapermen (presumably excluding himself), authors, and others, who lie for money, his lies were told not to be malicious or mischievous but merely to "amuse, instruct, and elevate without harm."

In Thompson & West's classic *History of Nevada,* published in 1881, writer Myron Angel (a former editor of both the *Reese River Reveille* and *The White Pine News* in Hamilton, NV), listed the qualities required to be a journalist in a Nevada mining camp, which he said included being "a good compositor, [and] a lively, versatile reporter, with imagination to fill columns in the absence of news."

Angel added, "The spirit of the Nevada press has always been an exaggerated character. . .aggressive to an extreme that not unfrequently resulted in a duel." He explained that since life in these mining communities was so full of events and activities that strained credulity, the reporters of the time "were an exaggerated aggregation that partook of and were an outgrowth of those excited times. Nothing in the ordinary would do." In Angel's mind, reporters had to "furnish literary food conditioned to digest by an inflated public mind, abnormally developed."

This meant that when there was a deficiency of "thrilling" news, reporters were then compelled to create news-masquerading, fanciful tales, which would titillate, confound, or captivate their readers. And when reporters tired of teasing these same readers, they would often turn their wicked pens on each other, according to Angel. Thus, there were feuds between various reporters, editors, and newspaper owners that were sometimes real but which were often ginned up to sell papers.

In this fertile soil bloomed a handful of frontier-hoax masters, including

Samuel L. Clemens, better known as Mark Twain, who called his made-up concoctions his "squibs"; William Wright, who wrote under the pen name Dan De Quille and who created what he called "quaints"; "Lying" Jim Townsend, who called his yarns "steamboats"; and longtime Nevada journalist Alfred Doten, who called his creations "sells." This inspired group also included Fred Hart, the creator of and "note-taker" for the Sazerac Lying Club; Carson City's Sam Davis, who actually invented a rival newspaper, the *Wabuska Mangler,* in order to carry on a fake feud; William J. Forbes, the peripatetic master of the pun and turn-of-phrase aficionado; and the largely forgotten Major John Dennis, who concocted a story about a phosphorus tree that was so believable, it appeared in the top scientific journals of his day.

All of this was, of course, genuine fake news—except everyone was in on the joke.

1

A Peculiar Relationship
with the Truth

*Nothing can now be believed which is seen in a newspaper. Truth
itself becomes suspicious by being put into that polluted vehicle.*

~ THOMAS JEFFERSON ~

ASSERTIONS ABOUT the proliferation of so-called fake news, largely promoted by political figures claiming that factual news accounts they
disagree with are not accurate or are untrustworthy, bring to mind past eras
when the lines between what was factual and what was fictional were frequently blurred.

Historically, newspapers have not been committed to providing objec-
tive coverage or to being fair or balanced. Until the mid-twentieth century,
American newspapers were generally vessels expressing the perspective of
the owner or publisher and were not seen as a tool for civic responsibility or
for representing the public interest. Indeed, even in the mid-twentieth century, journalist and media critic A. J. Liebling conveyed skepticism about
newspapers' objectivity, writing in *The New Yorker:* "Freedom of the press is
guaranteed only to those who own one."

Liebling was specifically speaking about newspaper industry consolida-
tion, which was still prevalent in 1960, but early newspapers, especially in
the nineteenth century, generally represented the views of whoever owned
the press, and their owners had no qualms about publishing whatever sold
more copies.

Historians generally believe that Benjamin Franklin, one of the nation's
Founding Fathers, concocted the first authentically fake news intended to
sway public opinion. In 1782, while serving in Paris as a representative of the
fledgling US government, Franklin decided that the best way to persuade

Europeans to side with the colonists (who would remain at war with the British until 1783) was to produce a fake issue of a real Boston newspaper.

Using a homemade press, Franklin created *Supplement to the Boston Independent Chronicle, Number 705, March 1782,* which included a letter allegedly written by a British officer. This letter graphically and falsely reported that Great Britain would be paying bounties to Native American tribes for the scalps of American men, women, and children. To make his propaganda appear more believable, Franklin included other real news articles and realistic-looking advertising in his broadsheet.

While Franklin clearly fabricated his *Supplement* for political purposes, many of the later so-called fake news creators had entirely different goals in mind: to entertain readers and to sell newspapers.

MAN-BATS ON THE MOON

An early example of this desire to entertain motivated a six-part series of articles that appeared in 1835 in *The New York Sun.* The recently launched, penny-daily newspaper claimed that a prominent astronomer, Sir John Herschel, had discovered life—and many other things—on the moon. The series kicked off on August 25 of that year by asserting that Herschel had made a number of startling and amazing discoveries while scrutinizing the moon from his observatory in South Africa.

The *Sun* presented the articles as being directly based on Herschel's discoveries, which allegedly had been reported first in the prestigious *Supplement to the Edinburgh Journal of Science.* The newspaper immodestly said that its series would describe "celestial discoveries of higher and more universal interest than any, in any science, yet known to the human race."

In the first installment, the *Sun* published a lengthy and, to the modern reader, somewhat tedious description of the amazing telescope that Herschel had purportedly developed to make his incredible finds. Readers, after wading through several column inches of scientific-sounding babble, finally got to the good stuff: accounts of a valley filled with waterfalls, rivers, and verdant flora and fauna as seen through this wonderous telescope.

"Innumerable cascades were bursting forth from the breasts of every one of these cliffs," the *Sun* recounted breathlessly. "At the foot of this boundary of hills was a perfect zone of woods. . . . Small collections of trees, of every imaginable kind, were scattered about the whole of this luxuriant area; and here our magnifiers blest our panting hopes with specimens of conscious existence."

Such descriptions only served to set up the next great discoveries. A few inches further into the story, readers learned that Herschel used his telescope to locate, within the forest, herds of brown, four-legged creatures, "having all the external characteristics of the bison, but more diminutive than any species of the bos genus in our natural history." These buffalo-like animals had semicircular horns, a hump on their shoulders, and were covered with thick, shaggy hair. They also had what the *Sun* described as a characteristic of all "lunar quadrupeds," which was a "remarkable fleshy appendage over the eyes, crossing the whole breadth of the forehead and united to the ears."

Obviously, Herschel had one remarkable telescope, to be able to see such detail from 238,900 miles away.

From there, the story grew even more incredible, as the magic telescope revealed bluish-colored animals that resembled goats, but ones with a single horn in the center of their brows. According to the *Sun,* these animals were particularly gregarious and leapt about like antelope. Clustered around these creatures were various species of moon birds. Herschel dubbed this place the "Valley of the Unicorns."

The article recounted that the telescope, as it moved across the lunar landscape, revealed lakes, volcanoes, and desolate valleys, before it uncovered another area "fertile to excess." In this location, Herschel claimed to be able to identify thirty-eight species of forest trees and twice as many other plants. He classified nine different species of mammals (somehow, remarkably, he was able to determine that they were warm-blooded vertebrates), including smaller versions of "rain-deer, the elk, the moose, the horned bear, and the biped beaver." The latter apparently resembled the common beaver on Earth, except it preferred to walk upright like a man. Still later, he described another four-legged creature with a long neck (a lunar giraffe?) but with the head of a sheep (should it then have been called a sheraffe?), spiral horns, and the torso of a deer (or maybe a deersheeraffe?).

But perhaps Herschel's most astounding discovery was seeing huge flocks of four-foot-tall, large, winged creatures. "We counted three parties of these creatures, of twelve, nine, and fifteen in each, walking erect towards a small wood near the base of the eastern precipices. Certainly they *were* like human beings, for their wings had now disappeared, and their attitude in walking was both erect and dignified. . . . We scientifically denominated them the Vespertilio-homo, or man-bat."

After reporting the sensational news about man-bats on the moon in the fifth part of the series, the paper's final installment revealed the existence of an apparently abandoned, pyramid-shaped temple built of polished sapphire, with a roof seemingly made of a yellow metal, "subdivided, curbed, and separated, so as to present a mass of violently agitated flames. . .enclosing a large sphere of a darker kind of metal."

What was the purpose of this temple? The *Sun* claimed that Herschel and his associates declined to speculate about its purpose.

The figures behind the *Sun's* moon hoax stories, as they became known, were Richard Adams Locke, who wrote the series, and the paper's printer and publisher, Benjamin Day. The latter is generally recognized as the founder of the "penny press," newspapers that targeted a mass audience rather than elite readers, cost a penny, and were often filled with sensationalized news stories. Day had started publishing the *Sun* on September 3, 1833, primarily as a vehicle to promote his printing business.

Locke's 17,000-word series jump-started the *Sun's* circulation, which had hovered around 8,000 that summer. Writing in the *Journal of English and American Studies,* historian István Kornél Vida says that the *Sun's* paid circulation soared to 19,360 within a few days of the first installment, making it one of the top-selling newspapers in the world at that time.

In an era when copyright laws were lax, the story was republished or written about in newspapers around the world. Rival publications, such as *The New York Times,* even conceded that the stories were "probable and possible."

According to Vida, within a couple of weeks of the series being published, its veracity finally began to be questioned. Another rival paper, *The New York Herald,* printed a column that called the entire series a hoax, and other skeptics soon followed suit. The *Sun,* however, never admitted that the stories were fake. Vida says that Locke, who publicly denied writing the stories, did later reveal to friends that his intention was to write a satire, not to deceive the public.

Edgar Allan Poe's Flight of Fancy

Regardless of Locke's true intentions, the fact remains that a believable hoax was good business for a newspaper. That became even more evident eight years later, when famed writer Edgar Allan Poe participated in his own version of stretching the truth in two different publications. In the June 18, 1843, issue of *The Spirit of the Times* newspaper, Poe, writing as "John Wise," teased a preview of his hoax when he wrote that a well-known balloonist would be attempting a transatlantic balloon flight in the summer of

1844. He followed up with a story, now known as the "Balloon Hoax," that appeared in the April 13, 1844, edition of *The New York Sun*—the same paper that had published Locke's story—under the headline *"ASTOUNDING NEWS!"*

In his piece, Poe, who had not yet begun to explore horror fiction and who was primarily working as a journalist covering science-related stories, asserted that a party of eight men had, amazingly, flown across the Atlantic Ocean in a balloon in just three days. In the front-page article, Poe wrote of an "aeronaut" named Monck Mason, who had led the team of explorers. Mason had allegedly developed the idea of an "Archimedean screw" device for propulsion that had powered the elliptical-shaped balloon from North Wales to South Carolina.

The story said that the party originally intended to fly from North Wales to Paris, but, due to a mechanical problem with the balloon's propeller (eventually fixed), compounded by particularly strong winds blowing in the opposite direction, the explorers decided to head to America.

"It was now that Mr. Ainsworth made an extraordinary, but to my fancy, a by no means unreasonable or chimerical proposition, in which he was instantly seconded by Mr. Holland—viz: that we should take advantage of the strong gale which bore us on, and in place of beating back to Paris, make an attempt to reach the coast of North America," noted an entry from Mason's fictional journal, which Poe quoted in the story.

Interestingly, Poe also wrote that the balloon, called "The Victoria," floated across the sea at an altitude of twenty-five thousand feet. This was the same altitude that the first successful, real-life, unpowered, human-carrying, transatlantic balloon flight (the "Double Eagle II") found was optimal during a six-day journey across the Atlantic in 1978.

Like the earlier Locke hoax, Poe's account was detailed in its description of landscapes and filled with plenty of technical information, including the specifics of the screw and rudder used for propulsion and steering, the size of the balloon, how much coal gas it required for lift, how much ballast was packed, the total amount of weight the balloon could bear, and a list of the supplies and equipment packed in the balloon's wicker car.

Also like the earlier hoax, Poe's story sold a lot of newspapers. The rival *New York Herald*, which immediately slammed the story as yet another *Sun* hoax, editorialized that the special edition of the *Sun* containing the story sold more than fifty thousand copies. "We think every intelligent reader will regard this attempt to hoax as not even possessing the character of pleasantry," the *Sun* opined.

A HOAX TO DISPROVE A HOAX

On October 18, 1869, the tiny town of Cardiff, NY—located about thirteen miles south of Syracuse—became the center of considerable attention when Syracuse newspapers announced in bold headlines: "A WONDERFUL DISCOVERY!...A NEW WONDER!...THE PETRIFIED GIANT!" The papers reported how, during the previous weekend, the body of a giant, petrified man had been uncovered on a Cardiff farm. Supposedly, men digging a well on William "Stub" Newell's farm had stumbled on the massive, stone remains. Newell and an associate, George Hull, quickly erected a large, white tent over the site of the stone Goliath and began charging admission.

Boosted by the breathless newspaper coverage, the giant, which measured ten feet, four and a half inches, and weighed nearly three thousand pounds, was an immediate sensation, attracting hundreds of curious visitors daily, who paid fifty cents to view him. Eventually, Newell and Hull sold the stone man to a group of prominent Syracuse citizens (for the amazing amount of $30,000), who had him moved to their community for exhibition. At the time, Syracuse was a young, up-and-coming city looking to put itself on the map. Not surprisingly, among the biggest boosters of the giant were the hometown newspapers.

Recognizing a good opportunity to take a poke at a rival community, *The New York Herald* published a letter on October 25, 1869, said to have been written by a local man named Thomas H. Ellis, who insisted that the Cardiff Giant was a fake.

"I will not go into any details regarding the discovery, as your readers are all well acquainted with it, as my object in addressing you is to make an exposé of the whole transaction," Ellis wrote. He went on to describe how the giant was most likely a statue created to "make money and perpetuate an enormous fraud upon the community."

Ellis said his proof was the fact that the statue, as he called it, had been uncovered by workers digging a well a few yards behind a barn, which was far too close to the structure for a well. He also said that the diggers had first encountered the statue's feet, then had somehow known to dig near its head, "thus knowing where to find the head." His final evidence was that he knew of a French Canadian stonecutter named Jules Géraud, who worked in local quarries. "Géraud was a monomaniac. His one idea was that he was an artist destined to rival the fame of Michael Angelo [*sic*]."

Ellis said that Géraud stayed in a shanty and never allowed anyone inside. Passersby, however, would often report hearing the sound of a mallet and chisel and were often curious about what Géraud was doing. A man named George Hooker, who had worked with Géraud in the quarries, noticed that his colleague had not been coming to work and stopped to check on him. He found the stonecutter in a feverish state and brought him food and medicine, hoping to help him recover.

But Géraud took a turn for the worse. According to Ellis (who had a sworn statement from Hooker), just before Géraud died, he told Hooker to pull back a curtain that revealed a statue of a giant, stone man, which he said was the image of St. Paul. Hooker himself then contracted pneumonia and, on his own death bed, revealed all of this information to Ellis and a doctor. Ellis also reported that five days after Géraud's death, his shanty burned down. Soon after, a mysterious stranger appeared, hired a wagon, and was seen taking an eleven-foot box to the Newell farm. Hooker said that after the fire he had walked to the spot where Géraud's cabin had once stood, expecting to find the statue of St. Paul in the ruins, but had found nothing. Ellis said that all of these curious facts, combined with Newell's refusal to allow the stone man to be examined by credible experts, added up to a fraud being perpetrated on the public.

Ellis's compelling letter caused an uproar, but it was also a hoax. The letter was the work of a nameless staffer at *The New York Herald*. The newspaper, however, was on to something. When the giant was finally subjected to scientific scrutiny, it became clear that it was a fake.

In December 1869, O. C. Marsh, chair of paleontology at Yale College, publicly questioned the giant's authenticity. With just a little bit of smugness, *The New York Herald* published an item with the headline "Professor Marsh, of Yale College, Pronounces It a Humbug." In the story, the newspaper reported that Marsh had recently examined the Cardiff Giant and had written a letter to a friend outlining why he thought the stone giant was fake.

"From such a source opinions are entitled to great weight on such a subject, and it must be admitted that the testimony of Professor Marsh finally settles the claim of the monstrosity to be of antique origin," noted the *Herald*.

In his letter, Marsh said that when he examined the giant, he could easily see that it was "of very recent origin, and a most decided humbug." He explained that it was cut from a block of gypsum, similar to the type found in that region, and that he could see the tool marks on the stone. He concluded, "Altogether the work is well calculated to impose upon the general public, but I am surprised that any scientific observation should not have at once detected the unmistakable evidence against the antiquity."

Within a short time, Hull stepped forward to acknowledge that the whole affair had been a scam. In a statement, he admitted "his part and complicity" in the fraud. He explained how it had all started several years earlier, when he had gotten into a heated dispute with a Reverend Turk over the literal meaning of a biblical passage indicating that "there were giants on the earth in those days." To prove his point that such a notion was absurd, Hull had decided to challenge religious literalists, like Reverend Turk, with a practical joke that would mock such beliefs and, of course, allow him to profit from the experience. He had hired a Chicago stonecutter to sculpt his giant from a five-ton hunk of Iowa gypsum. He had used a variety of techniques to give the statue the appearance of having skin pores and had rubbed the stone with sulfuric acid to give it an antique appearance.

He had also selected a location for burying the giant, remote and rural central New York, that was already fertile ground for those who were open to nontraditional religious and spiritual beliefs. It was in a part of New York State sometimes referred to as "the psychic highway," a region that had been home to Mother Ann Lee's apocalyptic Shaker sect in the late 1700s to early 1800s; to the messianic cult of Jemima Wilkinson in the early 1800s; to the three Fox sisters, who had played an important role in the creation of spiritualism in the mid-1800s; and to Joseph Smith, the founder of the Church of Jesus Christ of Latter-day Saints, who had said that he had received the Golden Tablets from the Angel Moroni in this area in 1823.

In the end, the Cardiff Giant became a term synonymous with great American hoaxes. The big stone man passed through a number of owners in subsequent years before the New York State Historical Association purchased it in 1948, deciding that the sculpture, at nearly eighty years old, had become an important historical oddity. It remains on display in The Farmers' Museum in Cooperstown, NY.

"A Shocking Sabbath Carnival of Death"

It should come as no surprise that another of the most famous hoaxes of the nineteenth century was perpetrated on readers by none other than *The New York Herald.* On November 9, 1874, the *Herald* published a front-page story that proclaimed, "Awful Calamity. . . Terrible Scenes of Mutilation. . . A Shocking Sabbath Carnival of Death."

What followed such a provocative headline was a chilling, first-person account of wild animals from New York's Central Park Zoo, who had allegedly escaped from their pens and viciously attacked local citizens. "Another Sunday of horror has been added to those already memorable in our city annals," the article said. "The list of mutilated, trampled and injured in various ways must reach nearly 200 persons of all ages, of which, so far as known, about sixty are very serious, and of these latter three can hardly outlast the night."

The *Herald* reported that the calamity had started when one of the zoo-keepers, a man named Chris Anderson, had begun relentlessly poking a rhinoceros with a cane. The angry animal had crashed out of his cage and had attacked his tormentor, "[had] knocked him down with a touch of his shoulder, and in an instant [had] trampled him out of recognition." The animal had then proceeded to pierce the dead man's body with his great horn, "dashing the last possible spark of life against the walls of one of the pens, which likewise gave way."

From there, the rampaging rhino supposedly had smashed open many of the other animal pens, allowing the lions, tigers, wolves, giraffes, bears, leopards, jaguars, hyenas, and other predators to go free, wandering out of the zoo and running wild through the streets of New York City. Finally, the humans had fought back, subduing the animals. A group of Swedish hunters had succeeded in shooting a lioness. A Dr. F. A. Thomas had used his saber to cut off the head of an escaped anaconda. A Bengal tiger had been shot to death by New York governor John A. Dix. And a bartender had clubbed a hyena to death. It was a gruesome story with tragic consequences—the paper listed the names of thirty-two human casualties and another eighteen who had supposedly been injured.

"Of the number actually killed it will be impossible to tell for some days. Of those wounded no full list can be ascertained. The charge of the savage beasts was the most unexampled in the history of cities. They tore through the leading thoroughfares with all the freedom they might have enjoyed in the native wilds," the author said.

A few lines down, the *Herald* writer did come clean, admitting to anyone who had read to the end of the lengthy tome: "Of course, the entire story given above is a pure fabrication. Not one word of it is true. Not a single act or incident described has taken place. It is a huge hoax, a wild romance, or whatever other epithet of utter untrustworthiness our readers may choose to apply to it." The writer then acknowledged that he had crafted the piece to make a point—that the Central Park Zoo kept its animals in "horrid" conditions. "A little oversight, a trifling imprudence might lead to the actual happening of all, and even worse than has been pictured," he concluded.

While observant readers could clearly identify the story as a hoax, many of them did not read the article to the end and believed that it was true. Traumatized residents of New York reportedly lined up on the docks to board ferries that would take them away from the city. The rival *New York Times* huffed in an editorial: "No such carefully prepared story could appear without the consent of the proprietor or editor—supposing that this strange newspaper *has* an editor, which seems rather a violent stretch of the imagination."

The man responsible for the story's publication was the *Herald*'s editor and owner, James Gordon Bennett Jr., who had inherited the paper from his father. The elder Bennett was a native of Scotland who had immigrated to the United States in 1820 at the age of twenty-four. After working briefly as a schoolteacher and later as a proofreader and bookseller in Boston, he had arrived in New York City in 1823 and had found work as a newspaper reporter and editor. Believing that he could produce a better product than most of the papers in New York at the time, he had scrounged together $500 and had started *The New York Herald* in 1835.

Bennett Sr.'s penny paper had been different from others in that he had not accepted political patronage money to survive—a standard practice at the time—and he had believed it was possible to produce an independent paper that relied on advertising support and a wide circulation. He also had introduced several editorial innovations that were soon copied by his competitors, such as hiring a dedicated financial reporter, who covered Wall Street and public listings of stocks; using woodcut illustrations (the technology for photos didn't yet exist); and maintaining a laser-like focus on issues of the day that appealed to average New Yorkers.

"Our only guide shall be good, sound, practical common sense, applicable to the business and bosoms of men engaged in everyday life," he had written in the first issue. "It is equally intended for the great masses of the community—the merchant, mechanic, working people—the private family as well as the public hotel—the journeyman and his employer—the clerk and principal."

Such a pledge, not surprisingly, had meant that Bennett would soon "dip deep in the muck of public and private filth in [his] mad scramble for circulation," as his biographer, Oliver Carlson, wrote in *The Man Who Made News: James Gordon Bennett.*

The result had been a growing circulation boosted by the coverage of sensational crime stories, public feuds with rival newspapers, immigration (yes, it was a hot-button issue even then), political corruption, and other tasty topics. In 1866, the elder Bennett, who had become one of the richest men in New York, turned over control of the paper to his son and retired.

Bennett Jr. had an even more keenly developed sense of the public's appetites than his father had. One of his favorite ways to produce entertaining news was to send a reporter around the world to interview compelling or controversial public figures, such as Napoleon III or German chancellor Otto von Bismarck. He famously sent reporter Henry Stanley to seek out the explorer and missionary Dr. David Livingstone in remote Central Africa. At the time of Bennett Jr.'s death in 1918, *The Washington Post* reported that he had once demanded that his editors come up with a "sensation" every day and had jokingly suggested that if no news were to be found, then he would have to have a reporter kill someone.

One of Bennett Jr.'s editors, T. B. Connery, wrote in *Harper's Magazine* in 1893 that he had concocted the basic idea for the fabricated zoo story after walking through Central Park one day and seeing the zookeepers almost lose control of a leopard that they were transferring from a carriage to a cage. He thought the paper should do something to draw attention to the poor operating conditions at the zoo:

> My object was entirely good—to warn the public and the authorities of an impending danger. My first impulse was to call public attention to the accident and to give the menagerie men a sound scolding through the columns of the American Thunderer; but I thought better of it. What would be the use of a little scolding and a few warnings? The menagerie men would only be a little more careful for a while, and then relapse into their old habits.
>
> That night in bed the idea came to me—get up a harmless little hoax, with just enough semblance of reality to give a salutary warning. That was what occurred to me, and the idea grew fast and furious, especially the fun of it, and I jotted down quickly the headings of my hoax to give to one of the reporters to develop and embellish.

Connery assigned two reporters to flesh out his hoax. Harry O'Conner wrote the first draft, which Connery found too broad in its humor and not believable enough. So, he handed it to another reporter, Joseph I. C. Clarke, who crafted a narrative filled with "ghastly and lifelike" details that would immediately catch the readers' attention.

Connery said he was shocked and surprised that so few people read the story to the end and didn't realize that the piece was fake. "To my shame be it confessed, I was utterly blind to the serious side of the hoax," he admitted.

MEANWHILE, OUT WEST

Considering such historical precedents, it would not have been out of place for a newspaper, especially in frontier Nevada, to concoct its own style of fake news that satirized local events or people. Pioneer Nevada was a creation of strivers, men and women (but mostly men) who were looking for a better life, wealth, and freedom. The pathway to those things for men was usually through mining or commerce. The former, with its promises of immense riches, was also the more difficult. Mining was a dangerous, dirty, and back-breaking business. Commerce was less physically taxing but, if you sought to set up your own business, required having capital or procuring investors, accepting a high level of risk, having an aptitude for numbers, and maintaining a strong work ethic. If you were a clever person with a talent for expressing yourself on paper, working at a newspaper offered yet another option for making a living.

The men (again, it was almost always men) who gravitated to the journalism world in Nevada might best be described as creative dreamers. Nearly all originally came to the state with big dreams of striking it rich in mining, but they soon realized that their future path would not be paved with silver or gold.

One such example was the young Samuel Clemens. In 1861, after traveling by stagecoach from Missouri to Carson City with his brother, Orion (who had been appointed to serve as secretary to Nevada's new territorial governor, James Nye), Clemens headed to the mining camps of Unionville and Aurora before he found a new line of work at Virginia City's *Territorial Enterprise*. It was a similar story for William Wright, who journeyed from Iowa to California in search of gold, then prospected in the Sierra Nevada foothills and Mono Lake area before unsuccessfully laboring in the Comstock's silver fields, and, eventually, also gravitated to the *Enterprise*. And it was the same for Fred Hart, who toiled on claims in Austin and Hamilton before picking up a pen and finding his voice in central Nevada's newspapers.

Nevada's early journalists sometimes also fabricated hoaxes. But why did the newspaper hoax find such a ready audience at this time in Nevada? The simple answer is that it was entertaining. For many people working in Nevada's mining camps, especially for men actually laboring in the mines, life was hard and unforgiving. As a result, they sought out diversions like brothels, saloons, gambling halls, and, perhaps, even a local newspaper that could offer information as well as entertainment or amusement. That's why frontier Nevada newspapers not only printed news items but also published the occasional joke, pun, piece of poetry, or prose.

And for the frontier editor or reporter, what better way to fight the monotony of writing stories about petty crime, freight and stage arrivals, mining stock reports, local government activities, and the weather than by publishing something more satisfying, like a good-natured "squib"?

Of course, part of what made Nevada's frontier newspaper writers unique was that contrary to expectations that they were an uneducated, unsophisticated lot, they were remarkably literate, witty, and clever. According to Lawrence I. Berkove, who almost single-handedly resurrected the Sagebrush School genre of Nevada writers (more on him and the Sagebrush School in the following chapter), "The best of the Sagebrush writers were cultured individuals (although many were self-educated) who appreciated the nuances and effects achieved by the great authors of English, American, and world literature and took pride in being able to write well."

He added, "The Sagebrush authors did not invent the literary hoax, but they did nurture it into a high art."

That they did.

A Sidebar—Twentieth-Century Scientific Hoaxes

The newspaper hoax did not disappear entirely in the twentieth century. But unlike the genesis of fake news in the nineteenth century, the basis for many of these more modern prank stories was often an amateur adventurer or misguided scientist who claimed to have uncovered something fantastic and unexpected, prompting a local reporter to sensationalize and write uncritically about it.

Perhaps the most outrageous fake news story, which echoed some of the science-based hoaxes of *The New York Sun* or *The New York Herald*, was an article that appeared on the front page of the *Los Angeles Times* on January 29, 1934. Under the headline "Lizard Peolpe's [*sic*] Catacomb City Hunted," reporter Jean Bosquet shared an incredible story about how an engineer was sinking a shaft under Fort Moore Hill to uncover a "Lost City" apparently built by a race of technologically advanced "Lizard People."

According to the story, G. Warren Shufelt, a geophysical mining engineer, planned to sink a 250-foot shaft on property located on North Hill Street, overlooking Sunset Boulevard, Spring Street, and North Broadway. Shufelt told the paper that he had invented a "radio x-ray" device, which he claimed had revealed an underground, lizard-shaped "pattern of catacombs and vaults forming the lost city." Shufelt said that he had first learned about the Lizard People from Chief Greenleaf of the Hopi Native American tribe of Arizona.

"The Indian provided the engineer with a legend which, according to both men, dovetails exactly with what Shufelt says he has found," Bosquet reported. "According to the legend as imparted by Shufelt. . .the radio x-ray has revealed the location of one of three lost cities in the Pacific Coast, the local one having been dug by the Lizard People after the 'great catastrophe' which occurred about 5,000 years ago. This legendary catastrophe was in the form of a huge tongue of fire, which 'came out of the Southwest, destroying all life in its path.'" The underground city was built so that its residents could escape future fires.

Bosquet said that the tunnels had been created by the legendary Lizard People with the help of "powerful chemicals." The complex was apparently large enough to accommodate one thousand families and included tall buildings, in which the families were housed, as well as food storage chambers.

"I know I was over a pattern of tunnels," Shufelt told the *Times*, explaining what he had allegedly discovered prior to speaking with Chief Greenleaf. "And I had mapped out the course of the tunnels, the position of large rooms scattered along the tunnel route, as well as the position of deposits of gold, but I couldn't understand the meaning of it."

In the center of the city, according to the legend and to Shufelt, was a chamber containing gold tablets that were four feet long and fourteen inches wide. Engraved on the plates was "the recorded history of the Mayans and on one particular tablet, the southwest corner of which [was] missing, [was] to be found the 'record of the origin of the human race.'" Shufelt said that he had taken X-ray photos of thirty-seven golden tablets, which he planned to excavate.

The amazing part of Shufelt's story—and, yes, he was a real person and a real mining engineer—is that he was able to persuade the Los Angeles

County Board of Supervisors that his radio X-ray machine had, indeed, revealed these long-hidden catacombs under the city and that the board should give him permission to start digging his shaft on Fort Moore Hill. The story was briefly followed by the *Times* and reported by the Associated Press. Apparently, after reaching the 250-foot level and finding nothing, Shufelt's funding dried up, the project was abandoned, and the media lost interest.

A similar tale of an amazing discovery appeared on the front page of the *San Francisco Examiner* on August 17, 1924. Under a giant headline—"Was the Garden of Eden Located in Nevada?"—the *Examiner* reported that geologist and engineer Captain Alan Le Baron claimed that he had stumbled on the actual Garden of Eden, apparently located in a remote valley about thirty miles south of Yerington, NV. There, he had discovered piles of large boulders and stones carved with hundreds of symbols, unusual writing, and images of prehistoric animals. He said the grounds around the rock art were littered with the bones of ancient camels, elephants, and lions.

Le Baron said that he had learned of the site, which he had named "Cascadia," from a Nevada prospector. After he had studied the carvings, he had become convinced that they were identical to Egyptian or Babylonian characters. Le Baron said that he had taken photos and had made drawings of the site and then had brought them to scholars in Egypt, who had agreed with his assessment. "The writings have been checked by every method at my command and I am prepared to say positively that this is not the work of Indians," he told the paper.

Le Baron's good fortune was in taking his discovery to the William Randolph Hearst–owned *Examiner,* which agreed to underwrite a full expedition to the site. Hearst papers at the time were known for their sensational, so-called "Yellow Journalism," so pursuing this story was an ideal undertaking. In spring 1924, Le Baron led a group that included Edward Clark, the *Examiner's* Sunday editor, and Dr. H. R. Fairclough, professor of classical literature at Stanford University. "We have found what appears to be the evidence of the oldest civilization in the world—the oldest writing, the oldest art, the oldest sacrifice, the oldest worship, and the oldest burial," Clark wrote. He said the expedition party had discovered the trail of a primitive culture that would prove that the "white race had its origin somewhere in western America."

Wanting to wring as much publicity as possible out of its investment in the expedition, the *Examiner* filled its entire August 17 front page, along with several inside pages, with coverage of the findings. Clark also crafted a self-congratulatory editorial in which he praised the paper's role in financing the survey and celebrated all of the alleged discoveries. The paper followed up with more stories on August 18 and August 19, which featured large, black-and-white photos of the rock carvings and boasted sensational headlines: "Nevada Carvings Are Like Egyptian Hieroglyphs" and "The 'Hill of a Thousand Tombs,' Ancient Burial Site." The latter story also featured a chart indicating (falsely) that the Nevada rockwriting was nearly identical to hieroglyphics. Adjacent to that coverage, Clark quoted a professor of anatomy at the University College of London, who was an expert on mummies and who said that he recognized similarities between the Nevada writing and the glyphs of both ancient Babylonians and Egyptians.

"Paradise regained!" Clark enthusiastically wrote in the opening paragraph of his August 19 story. He continued by stating that the fact that there were so many images of the sun on the stones was proof that the site was a place of worship. He added that the presence of so many animal drawings was further evidence that the site was a place where many animals were sacrificed to some prehistoric gods. For his part, Le Baron, who had spent years in Egypt studying the pyramids, told Clark that he had been able to partially translate the carvings, which he claimed "said in effect that three hundred young people had returned to the site and it was the burial place of the fathers."

Le Baron also said he was convinced that all of the thousands of boulders on the surrounding hills sat atop tombs. At one point, he directed workers to dig a shaft on the flat, sandy ground between the base of the hill and the nearby East Walker River. As might be expected, after they had dug about thirty feet, groundwater filled the tunnel, and they abandoned the effort. Le Baron further told Clark that if the group simply dug under each boulder, they would encounter human remains. "We removed the stones and started digging beneath them with a prospector's pick and our bare hands. Beneath the layers of brown stones we found sand and suddenly the blue-grayness changed to a yellowish white," Clark wrote. He said the yellow-colored dirt was the "dust of a human dead longer than any scientist dare guess." Letting the yellow soil fall between his fingers and blow from the palm of his hand, he said that the experience was "one of indescribable awe."

Adventurers and scientists weren't the only ones who embraced the discovery. A 1925 issue of *Theosophy* magazine also applauded the findings. The

magazine was published by the Theosophical Society, a religious organization that melded Eastern and Western religions with a dash of mysticism,
reincarnation, and a belief in the existence of the lost island of Atlantis.
Celebrating their belief that the findings "suddenly cut the Gordian knot
by providing a new center of racial origin," *Theosophy* declared that the rock
carvings were said to be identical in form to symbols found in Egyptian,
Chaldean, Babylonian, Chinese, and Arabic writing and that they proved
the "validity of the Wisdom-Religion [said to be the ancient root religion
of Theosophy]."

As for Le Baron, he managed to remain a celebrity for a little while.
Described as a charming, good-looking man, he was able to woo and marry
a local schoolteacher, Georganne Kaufman, although the union was not
long-lived. By the late 1930s, he had largely disappeared from the public eye
and was reportedly last seen working as a member of a road crew building
the highway between Yerington and Fernley.

Later experts who studied the rock art at Cascadia concluded that they
were not ancient Egyptian or Babylonian hieroglyphics but Native American petroglyphs, created by the same people disparaged by Le Baron. Bones
and other fossil fragments found around the boulders turned out to be from
indigenous sheep, deer, and rabbits.

In the end, the story of the Garden of Eden being found in Nevada
was—like the report of Lizard People and a lost city beneath Los Angeles—
simply fun but fake news.

2

The Sagebrush School

*Their writing has a sense of high spirits, of tasting life at
its most flavorful, and of a camaraderie of soul mates.*

~ LAWRENCE I. BERKOVE ~

AUTHOR AND LITERARY historian Ella Sterling Cummins first coined
the term "Sagebrush School" to define a seminal group of nineteenth
century–Nevada journalists. In her 1893 book, *The Story of the Files: A Review
of Californian Writers and Literature* (which also includes a chapter on
Nevada authors), she ascribed the name to a dozen or so writers, including
Mark Twain, Dan De Quille, and Fred Hart, who were part of a creative
movement that began at Virginia City's *Territorial Enterprise* newspaper,
under the tutelage of editor Joseph T. Goodman.

"Sagebrush School? Why not?" she wrote. "Nothing in all our Western
literature so distinctly savors of the soil as the characteristic books written
by the men of Nevada and that interior part of the State where the sagebrush grows." Cummins went on to say that there must be something in the
region that compelled such talented writers to forsake writing about beautiful things and to devote their pens to "that weird, fascinating, ugly land in
which they dwelled."

Cummins noted that the *Enterprise* was where readers first discovered
Mark Twain and his "lucubrations before he became famous to the rest of
the world, but was a welcome and familiar jester with cap and bells to the
people of Nevada."

Her admiration for the collective literary might of the Comstock's
chroniclers—and her role in defining them as an important group—
remained largely forgotten until an academic named Lawrence I. Berkove
began a deep dive into their nearly forgotten works. Berkove, who died in
2018, was a professor of English and American literature at the University

of Michigan–Dearborn for more than four decades, and his own interest in these writers was brought to light by Cheryll Glotfelty, a retired professor of literature and the environment at the University of Nevada, Reno.

Glotfelty shone a light on all this scholarship when she wrote an insightful article on Berkove for the fall 2008 issue of the *Nevada Historical Society Quarterly*. She traced the literature professor's interest in the Sagebrush School writers to the early 1960s, when Berkove was pursuing his PhD at the University of Pennsylvania. While serving as a teaching assistant, he oversaw the work of a student who wrote a paper on nineteenth century–California writer Ambrose Bierce. The student earned an A for the work, but Berkove noticed that the paper was light on research citations. When he tried to find other resources that might have been available to the student, he discovered that very little scholarly work had been done on Bierce. As a result, Berkove was inspired to write his dissertation on this author, who had written both *The Devil's Dictionary* and *An Occurrence at Owl Creek*.

Glotfelty writes, "When Berkove showed his advisor his first chapter, the advisor noticed that some of Bierce's stories had originally been published in the *San Francisco Examiner*, and he asked Berkove if he had consulted the original texts." After Berkove said that he had not, the advisor suggested that he do so. In response, Berkove began examining microfilm and visiting the Library of Congress to read the stories in their original versions. As he combed through various newspapers and periodicals, he not only became aware of differences between the reprinted versions and the originals, but he also noticed other nineteenth-century writers who displayed impressive literary skills, and he developed a particular fascination for a gifted Virginia City journalist named Dan De Quille.

Berkove's subsequent research into De Quille led him to discover the connection between De Quille and Mark Twain and, ultimately, to wonder about additional Nevada writers who might have influenced Twain during his time in the Silver State. As Glotfelty explains, "Berkove discovered a group of other writers who, with Twain, constituted a vibrant and distinctive literary school which an 1893 study by Ella Sterling Cummins had dubbed the Sagebrush School. Adopting the name for the movement that Cummins had coined, Berkove came to realize that in their own era, members of the Sagebrush School were not minor writers. They were some of the most respected writers of the day, and they went on to prominent careers."

Glotfelty notes that Berkove wrote about the influence these writers had on Twain's development, including introducing him to the idea of the literary hoax. In his 2006 book, *The Sagebrush Anthology: Literature from the Silver Age of the Old West,* Berkove asserted, "[The fact that] humor and hoaxing were practically ubiquitous in Sagebrush literature is, in itself, an important clue to the pervasive and deep influence of the Sagebrush style on Mark Twain."

This opinion is shared by folklorist and Nevada historian Ronald M. James, who writes that when Samuel Clemens arrived in Nevada in 1862, "The tradition of the Western Tall Tale was not yet part of his tool-kit." James says that Clemens (who adopted the Mark Twain pen name in 1863) quickly learned the art of the hoax under "the guidance of the best in Virginia City, where he found a good use for the 'stretchers' he was fond of telling in Missouri. Inducted into a well-established literary school of the West, Clemens absorbed new ideas that helped him become a lauded American author."

An Exclusive Club

Just who were the members of the Sagebrush School? Ella Sterling Cummins, who mostly focused on nineteenth century–California writers in *The Story of the Files,* also generously paid tribute to some of Nevada's early scribes. On her list of talents were the obvious choices, such as Mark Twain and Dan De Quille, as well as some lesser-known writers, including Joseph Goodman, Fred Hart, Henry Rust Mighels, Sam Davis, John Franklin Swift, C. C. Goodwin, Joseph Wasson, and Rollin M. Daggett. While most had journalism experience, several on her list earned a place because of their skills in writing fiction, poetry, or plays.

Cummins's criteria for inclusion in the Sagebrush School were a bit quirky and perhaps reflected the fact that in the late nineteenth century, the boundaries between California and Nevada—unresolved until 1980!—were somewhat fluid. Thus, she included John Franklin Swift, who had never lived in the Silver State but who had spent nearly his entire life in San Francisco. Swift made her list because several of his best-known fictional works, such as *Robert Greathouse: A Story of the Nevada Silver Mines,* were set in Nevada. Similarly, Joseph Wasson, who is largely associated with California politics (having represented Mono County, CA, in the state legislature), made her list because he established a well-regarded newspaper in Winnemucca, NV, *The Winnemucca Argent,* which he published briefly in 1868 from July to November. In addition to his political success, Wasson had an outstanding journalism career, which included working as an international correspondent in Europe for a few years and owning a newspaper in Arizona.

The rest of Cummins's inductees into the Sagebrush School, however, clearly lived and breathed Nevada's sage-scented air, even if their time in the state was not permanent. Cummins recounted an anecdote involving Mark Twain, who, she said, was a millionaire for ten days once in the mining camp of Aurora. Twain and a friend had discovered a rich lode, which they named "The Wide West," but upon returning to their camp, neither bothered to record paperwork for the claim within the ten-day window allowed for such filings. By the time they returned to their claim, it was overrun by other prospectors with proper claims. "Thus fell his hopes, and, instead of a mining millionaire, a humorist was spared to the world," she wrote.

Cummins was equally generous in describing other writers, including Henry Rust Mighels, author of *Sagebrush Leaves,* a book of essays, letters, humorous sketches, and articles that his widow published shortly after he died in 1879. Nellie Verrill Mighels used the proceeds from the book to help defray her husband's medical and funeral expenses. Henry Mighels was also editor and publisher of the *Carson Appeal* newspaper from 1865 until his death. As an aside, and to illustrate the close-knit nature of the Nevada journalism community, Henry and Nellie's son, Philip, was Ella Sterling Cummings's second husband; and Nellie eventually married Sam Davis, another member of the Sagebrush School, who would edit the *Appeal* from 1880 to 1898.

It was up to Berkove—who placed the heyday of these writers as being, roughly, from 1859 to 1914—to expand the school's roster to include Alfred Doten, James W. Gally, Arthur McEwen, Denis E. McCarthy, James "Lying Jim" Townsend, Thomas Fitch, and Sarah Winnemucca. While long overlooked and underestimated, the Sagebrush School, according to Berkove, was more than worthy of study and recognition because of the rare talent and ability found among its members.

"Its authors had diverse and interesting lives apart from their connections with Twain, pursued purposes and goals of their own, and merit recognition for having achieved literary successes independent of Twain," he wrote.

Berkove acknowledged that the Sagebrush School was largely a creation of twentieth century–literary critics and academics and that it was not a formal literary club or movement at the time when its members were writing, although many of them were contemporaries and knew each other. Still, he said, the group was unique, with their name serving as "the best way to describe the small but remarkable constellation of authors who were inspired by their immersion in the unique atmosphere of Nevada's first mining boom to produce excellent and memorable literature under conditions seemingly inimical to art."

Another observer who recognized the special qualities of the Silver State's scribes was folklorist Duncan Emrich, who, in 1950, published *Comstock Bonanza,* a collection of the writings of Twain and De Quille, as well as pieces by J. Ross Browne, Davis, Gally, Goodman, Hart, and Bret Harte.

Emrich, who served as head of the Archive of Folk Song at the Library of Congress from 1945 to 1955, said that he had selected his roster of writers because they had either lived in the Comstock region at one time, had spent some time there, or had "[drawn] from it and from one another much of the inspiration for their work." He noted that the subject matter of the stories in his anthology was not restricted to Virginia City but also included other parts of Nevada, as well as "spilling over the range of the Sierra to touch the Mother Lode country and San Francisco."

Emrich also recognized a key characteristic that made members of the Sagebrush School so identifiable: their ability to convey "fun" in their work. "The writers wrote for their mining-camp audiences to give their readers enjoyment. Fun. Something for the whole camp to laugh over. This Nevada fun was not—as frequently is the case with humor—mocking, caustic, satirical, sentimental, or superior. The writers included themselves in the fun, were not divorced from it," he noted.

And he pointed out yet another attribute of these writers—their focus on frontier individualism, independence, and the "democratic tone" of mining camp societies. He said that the Sagebrush scribes frequently depicted a land that was fairly egalitarian. Additionally, their work often pointed out, at times humorously, instances of political favoritism, societal injustice, or corruption. "There was no inhibiting veneer of civilization, no stratification of society, no fixed patterns to warp the individual out of his true shape," he wrote. "Their writings, in general, poked fun at, rather than had fun with, the people about whom they wrote."

In 2019 Nevada historical writer David W. Toll created the Nevada Hall of Fame on a popular travel website that he operated. Toll's list honored "individuals who. . .achieved fame here, or at least deserved to." He included yet another key figure, William J. Forbes, a largely forgotten newspaperman from the same era, who used clever word play and puns in his work and which he sometimes published under the name "Semblins."

Forbes, who is definitely worthy of being included as one of the Silver State's nineteenth-century satirists, worked at and/or owned about a dozen newspapers in California and Nevada in the 1860s and 1870s. The Nevada papers included the *Humboldt Register* in Unionville and Winnemucca, the *Daily Union* in Virginia City, and *Measure for Measure* in Battle Mountain.

Bret Harte's West

One additional name sometimes associated with the Sagebrush School is that of Bret Harte. He had no direct link to Nevada but can be considered an affiliated member of the group because he had close connections with several of the writers, particularly with those who eventually moved on from Nevada to San Francisco to seek new writing opportunities.

Harte, who was born Francis Bret Harte in Albany, NY, in 1836, is credited with the idea of incorporating western "local color" into story dialogue and setting (although Mark Twain, who later famously feuded with him, claimed that no one ever spoke in mining-camp lingo as written by Harte). After growing up in New York City and Brooklyn, Harte headed west in February 1854 with his younger sister to reconnect with their mother, who had remarried and who was living in Oakland, CA. He was seventeen years old.

Harte initially had little interest in gold mining, preferring his books to the hard labor of a mining camp. In the late 1850s, after working as a tutor, a teacher, and a surveyor, he found himself unemployed, and so he headed to the gold mines. At a place called Jackass Hill, Harte befriended a miner named Jim Gillis (who eight years later would become friends with Mark Twain) and tried his hand at panning for gold. After a short time, Gillis, recognizing that Harte was no miner, supposedly gave him a twenty-dollar gold piece and sent him back to San Francisco.

Despite having spent only about three months in California's gold rush camps, Harte was left with lasting impressions, and about a decade later, he would turn them into several of his best-known short stories, including "The Luck of Roaring Camp" and "The Outcasts of Poker Flat."

Once back in San Francisco, Harte was able to find work as a typesetter for *The Golden Era,* a small but well-regarded literary newspaper founded in 1852 by Rollin M. Daggett and J. MacDonough Foard. Harte also wrote columns, poems, and sketches for the paper for several years and eventually became its editor in 1860. In that latter role, he guided the paper in incorporating more literary content, and he published some early works by Twain, who was still employed at the *Territorial Enterprise* in Virginia City. In 1864, Harte helped establish a rival San Francisco literary newspaper, *The Californian,* and became its editor. While in that capacity, he hired Twain, who had recently left Nevada, as a reporter and columnist.

In the beginning, their relationship was productive and fruitful. As a staff writer, Twain was instructed to write a weekly newspaper article at a pay rate of fifty dollars per week. Several months into the arrangement, Twain headed to the Sierra Nevada foothills to stay with Jim Gillis on Jackass Hill. After three months there, he returned, bringing with him an armful of new stories and tall tales, including a humorous yarn about a jumping frog, which he immediately shared with Harte. The frog story had long circulated in mining camps, and a version of it had been published by Jim Townsend in 1853, but Twain was able to tell it in a way that was fresh and inventive.

The editor, as well as several other friends of Twain, encouraged him to write the frog story. In November 1865 the story, "Jim Smiley and His Jumping Frog," was published in the *New York Saturday Press,* a literary newspaper. The tale proved enormously popular and was republished in several other newspapers and magazines. Twain refined the story further for Harte's *Californian,* and that version, titled "The Celebrated Jumping Frog of Calaveras County," was printed in December 1865. Two years later, the story became the centerpiece of Twain's first book, *The Celebrated Jumping Frog of Calaveras County and Other Sketches.*

Twain thought so highly of Harte that in a letter to his mother, he wrote that while he generally thought of himself as being at the head of the "breed of scribblers" working in San Francisco, he believed that the honor "properly [belonged] to Bret Harte."

In 1866 Twain left *The Californian* to travel abroad for two years, gathering material that would become his next book. When he returned, he headed to San Francisco, where Harte generously assisted him in revising a manuscript that would become *The Innocents Abroad.* Several years later, Twain wrote to a friend that Harte had "trimmed and trained and schooled me patiently until he changed me from an awkward utterer of coarse grotesqueness to a writer of paragraphs and chapters that have found favor in the eyes of even some of the very decentest [*sic*] people in the land."

In 1868 Harte became editor of *The Overland Monthly*, a new San Francisco–based literary magazine, where he published his most popular works, including "The Luck of Roaring Camp," "Tennessee's Partner," and the satirical poem "Plain Language from Truthful James" (which became better known by its alternate title, "Heathen Chinee," and which alluded to prejudice against Chinese workers in Northern California). In 1871 he left the magazine and signed a one-year contract with *The Atlantic Monthly* in New York, which made him the highest paid writer in America ($10,000 per month for one story or poem). Distracted by his own fame, Harte had a difficult time keeping up with the contract's requirements, and the job was not extended beyond the year.

Harte never returned to California (spending the last seventeen years of his life in London), but he continued to rework the same gold-rush-era material (to varying degrees of success) in many of his stories for much of the rest of his life.

Twain and Harte's relationship soured over the years. In many accounts, the cause of the rift was a failed partnership between the two to co-author and produce a play in 1876 based on characters from their respective stories. The two were said to have had disagreements over money (Harte had a difficult time not spending it, and Twain—a terrible businessman—had a difficult time not losing it due to investing in money-losing ventures); and they were said to have quarreled over the play's direction. When they finally finished it, the play was a failure, despite its association with two of America's best-known writers.

Others have suggested that Harte, who had stayed for two weeks with Twain and his wife in 1876, may have insulted his hostess, Olivia Langdon Clemens, which would certainly have been another reason for the split. It is also known that Twain disapproved of the manner in which Harte spent money (recklessly), seemed to live off the generosity of others, and treated his own wife and children with seeming indifference (he did not live with them most of the time).

For the rest of his life, Twain rarely missed an opportunity to put down his former friend, whom he once described as a "liar, a thief, a swindler, a snob, a sot, a sponge, a coward, a Jeremy Diddler [a confidence man], he is brim full of treachery." In *Mark Twain's Autobiography*, he wrote: "In the early days I liked Bret Harte and so did the others, but by and by I got over it; so also did the others. He couldn't keep a friend permanently. He was bad, distinctly bad; he had no feeling and he had no conscience."

THE DEVIL'S TYPOGRAPHER

Besides Harte, the other seminal writer claiming a key affiliation with the Sagebrush School was Ambrose Bierce, the literary figure who first captured Berkove's interest. Just seven years younger than Twain (and six years younger than Harte), Bierce gained national fame as a syndicated newspaper columnist and as the author of a number of highly regarded short stories and books, including the macabre satire *The Devil's Dictionary*. He came along after Twain, De Quille, Harte, and others had already earned their reputations. Bierce's biographer, Carey McWilliams, however, wrote that "his first work clearly belonged to the school of Dan De Quille and Mark Twain."

McWilliams pointed out that Bierce arrived in San Francisco (in 1880) just as the era of Twain, De Quille, Harte, and their contemporaries was coming to an end. But their influence was still strong—they had crafted a voice that McWilliams described as "a typically Western manner of writing, aptly characterized by [twentieth-century Welsh writer] Idwal Jones as 'whimsical and bombastic.'" McWilliams said that that style, which the young Bierce mirrored, "was a child of the marriage of the wildly humorous manner of Mark Twain—the literary equivalent of a barroom story—with the plaintive and sentimental whimsicality of Bret Harte—an etherealized banjo tune."

Over time, of course, Bierce developed his own voice: a clear-eyed, sharp-tongued, witty but often-vicious style that would eventually earn him such sobriquets as "Bitter Bierce," the "Devil's Topographer," and "one of the biggest SOBS in American literature."

Bierce was born in a tiny settlement along Horse Cave Creek in Meigs County, Ohio, on June 24, 1842. The tenth of thirteen children, each of whom was given a name starting with an 'A' (Abigail, Amelia, Ann, Addison, Aurelius, Augustus, Almeda, Andrew, Albert, Ambrose, Arthur, Adelia, and Aurelia), Bierce grew up in Kosciusko County, Indiana, and attended a military school in Kentucky. In 1861 he enlisted in the Union Army and saw action numerous times, including in the Battle of Shiloh and in the Battle of Chickamauga.

In 1867 he moved to San Francisco, finding work as a night watchman for the US Mint in the city. While working at the mint, Bierce started writing satirical poetry and essays for *The Californian*, *The New Era*, and, later, for the *San Francisco News Letter and California Advertiser*, which were some of the city's better-known literary newspapers. By 1868 he had quit the mint and was serving as editor of the *News Letter*, a role that included writing a regular column. In a short time, Bierce's "Town Crier" became the talk of San Francisco, as he wrote savage takedowns of organized religion, local politicians, and rival newspapers.

While Bierce was often caustic and could be downright cruel in his criticism of other writers, he had a more measured relationship with Twain, who could be equally sarcastic when prompted or provoked. Twain generally spoke highly of Bierce and his work, and there appears to have been genuine, mutual respect between the two writers. Interestingly, Bierce also wrote fondly of Bret Harte, who was a rival editor at *The Overland Monthly* and at the peak of his creative output. In return, Harte published several of Bierce's more serious and contemplative essays (under the pen name Ursus).

Following a brief time in London and a failed attempt at mining in Deadwood, SD, Bierce returned to San Francisco journalism. In 1887 he was hired by William Randolph Hearst, owner of the *San Francisco Examiner*. It was the beginning of a long and successful relationship, with Bierce receiving a generous salary to write a column (which eventually went national), fiction (including "Occurrence at Owl Creek," his best short story), and poetry for the paper. He also reworked much of his literary output, publishing it in successful books, such as his best-known work, *The Devil's Dictionary*.

In late 1913 the seventy-one-year-old Bierce planned to embark on a quixotic journey to Mexico, which was in the midst of a civil war. He told friends that he intended to cover the revolution being led by Pancho Villa. Sometime in December, he is thought to have slipped into Mexico. He was never seen or heard of again.

RENAISSANCE MEN

Not all of the members of the Sagebrush School were satirists, humorists, or writers of hoaxes. Some, such as Gally, Wasson, and Winnemucca, primarily gained fame as writers of non-satirical fiction, poetry, drama, and memoir. Others, including Daggett, Davis, Wells Drury, Goodman, Goodwin, and McEwen, were successful journalists who also excelled in other literary arenas. For example, Sam Davis was not only a renowned newspaperman and a successful politician, but he also wrote well-regarded poetry and fiction, a two-volume history of Nevada, and a comic opera. Daggett and Goodman collaborated on a five-act play, *The Psychoscope*, and both wrote hundreds of poems, many of which were popular during their era.

Berkove, who rightly described the Sagebrush School's members as "Renaissance men," noted that while they may have been frontiersmen, they weren't uneducated. All came from other more-established parts of the country, like Ohio, Iowa, and New York. They were typically well read, with a knowledge of Milton, Shakespeare, Dante, Homer, and many of the classic works of English and European literature. That said, many of them excelled at humor and, according to Berkove, "raised the literary hoax to the level of high art."

Part of the reason they incorporated literary devices like the hoax into their writing, Berkove said, is because they all had strong, personal moral codes: notions about honor and doing the right thing. The mining environments in which they lived and wrote, which were unregulated and lacking in most of the trappings of law and order, made them skeptics of institutions, including the legal system and formalized religion.

"They supported fair play and equity more than legality," he said. "They inclined to the position that if a man had bedrock principles that were admirable and consistently upheld, he would be 'justified' in upholding his rights, even if it meant going against the system."

Berkove explained that the hoax was born of that philosophy. Mining get-rich scams (along with corrupted journalists, bribed public officials, wealthy and amoral mining magnates, and other injustices) were prevalent at the time because of the lack of a functional legal system. Berkove said that it was only natural that some journalists would begin to incorporate such subjects into their writing, often as a way to poke fun at the established order.

"The literary hoax deliberately misrepresents something at odds with fact—because it is untrue, impossible, or highly improbable—with the use of details intended to make it seem plausible," he wrote. "It also implicates the reader, who falls victim to the deceit by not reading carefully and thoughtfully. The hoax occupies the middle ground between a lie and a tall tale."

In 2009 the Nevada Writers Hall of Fame inducted the Sagebrush School, recognizing its special place in American literature. The hall's website notes: "Sagebrush writing reflects and often embellishes the Nevada experience of cosmopolitan mining booms, frontier justice, and harsh and dramatic landscapes. It is a principled literary movement that often reveals the writers' comradery. Sagebrush journalism upheld a code of honor in crusading against corruption and injustice."

Quoting Berkove, the hall concludes that the "characteristics of the Sagebrush School are a 'fascination with hoaxes, delight in wit, audacity, and an irreverent attitude towards inflated authority and outworn tradition.'. . . They were an extraordinary cast of characters who created a distinctive early voice in our national literature—with lasting (if hitherto unacknowledged) influence."

It was an honor that was long overdue.

3

The Humorist

Get your facts first, then you can distort them as you please.

~ MARK TWAIN (SAMUEL L. CLEMENS) ~

SAMUEL LANGHORNE CLEMENS was not always Mark Twain. Earlier in his writing career, he used other pseudonyms, including "W. Epaminondas Adrastus Perkins," "Epaminondas Adrastus Blab," "Thomas Jefferson Snodgrass," "Quintius Curtius Snodgrass," "Rambler," "Grumbler," "Peter Pencilcase's Son," "John Snooks," "Sergeant Fathom," and "Josh."

The use of pen names by journalists was fairly common in Twain's time. His close friend and coworker at Virginia City's *Territorial Enterprise,* William Wright, was far better known by his nom de plume, Dan De Quille. Another good friend, Charles Farrar Browne, who became one of Twain's mentors and who was himself a famed author and lecturer, was much better known by his pen name, "Artemus Ward."

Part of the appeal of using another name was that it offered authors the freedom to express what they might not be able or willing to say under their real name. Indeed, Andrew Hoffman, author of *Inventing Mark Twain,* proposes that "Twain" was actually a persona that Samuel Clemens adopted, first in print and then in person, that allowed him to say things he might be more reticent to say as himself.

"In my view, the greatest of all Clemens's accomplishments is his invention of Mark Twain. Twain was, and is, a nearly complete human being, constructed on a scale at the very edge of imagination," Hoffman writes. "Rather than make of Mark Twain someone entirely distinct from Sam Clemens, Clemens made him a near match. . . . He became two people occupying the same body: the brilliant, though acerbic, public man of letters known as Mark Twain; and the cowed, uncertain, and underdeveloped boy-man Sam Clemens."

In Nevada, however, Clemens had not yet created the Twain persona we know today—the clever man with the head of thick, bushy, white hair, with a drooping mustache, garbed in a white suit, who had the perfect quip for any occasion (see the late Hal Holbrook or Nevada's noted Twain imperson-ator, MacAvoy Layne, for that incarnation of Twain). Clemens was young, a bit cocky, and more than a little naïve. He did not arrive in Virginia City as a mature, developed talent but rather as a project—someone the newspa-pers' editors viewed as not quite developed as a writer but one who showed potential.

How It All Began

The story of how Sam Clemens came to work for the *Territorial Enterprise* is a key part of Mark Twain's origin story. Born in Florida, MO, in 1835, Clemens grew up in nearby Hannibal, MO. While still in his teens, he wrote and published a few pieces in the *Hannibal Journal,* which was owned by his older and more serious brother, Orion. Copies of the paper, redis-covered in the 1930s, show that in May 1853, while Orion was away for a time, Clemens published several poems and what *The New York Times* later described as "witty correspondence" between two of Clemens's earli-est invented personae, "The Rambler" and "The Grumbler." When Orion returned, however, he banished his brother from the editorial pages, noting in his own commentary, "Rambler and his enemies must stop this stuff."

Later, in 1856 and 1857, the *Keokuk* (Iowa) *Saturday Post,* based in a com-munity where Orion had set up a printing business, published three letters written by Clemens, who used the pseudonym Thomas Jefferson Snodgrass and described his travels in St. Louis and Cincinnati. Clemens received a payment of five dollars per letter, making the letters his first paid-journal-ism work. He wrote them in his region's vernacular—"Last night as I was a settin in the parlor of my Dutch boardin house in Fourth street (I board among the crouters so as to observe human natur in a forren aspeck)"—and they reflected his earliest attempts at writing the observational humor and sarcasm for which he would later become famous.

In 1861 Clemens, who was twenty-five years old at the time, joined Orion to travel from Missouri to Carson City, NV. Orion, who was an active member of Abraham Lincoln's Republican Party, had received a presi-dential appointment to serve as secretary to James W. Nye, governor of the newly created Nevada Territory (President James Buchanan had signed the law establishing the territory on March 2, 1861; President Lincoln made the initial officeholder appointments there). However, Orion did not have the funds to travel to his new job. Fortunately, his younger brother had managed to save about $1,200 from his time piloting stern-wheelers on the Mississippi River (he had quit this job with the advent of the Civil War, having no interest in serving in the ranks of either side during the conflict), and he offered to pay for Orion's transportation if he could tag along. In return, Orion promised to help his brother find a federal job, perhaps as an assistant to the territorial secretary.

The Clemens brothers embarked on their 1,900-mile stagecoach journey to Nevada on July 26, 1861, and they traveled through Nebraska, Wyoming, and Utah before reaching the Silver State. The pair, along with other traveling companions, arrived at Carson City, the seat of the new territorial government, on August 14, 1861.

Within a short time, it became obvious to Sam that there was no possibility of a federal job in Carson City, so he began to look around for other work. Eager to make something of himself, he first sought to become a lumber baron at Lake Tahoe and, with several companions, headed up to the lake to stake a claim on a portion of the region's lushly forested lands. That particular scheme came to a quick end after he left a campfire burning one night and torched several acres of trees.

Clemens then returned to Carson City, where his brother was able to procure him a temporary job as a clerk during the two-month-long session of the First Nevada Territorial Legislature. At the conclusion of the session, he joined three other companions to travel to a new mining boomtown called Unionville, located 175 miles northeast of Carson City. After a fruitless month of prospecting (and discovering that iron pyrite, or fool's gold, was not the same as real gold), he decided to head to another mining region that appeared more promising, the Esmeralda mining district at Aurora, located about 120 miles south of Carson City. Clemens and his brother apparently had invested in several claims in Aurora, so he thought this might be where he would finally make some money.

TRADING A PICKAX FOR A PEN

The Esmeralda district proved to be no more lucrative for Clemens than Unionville had. Running out of funds, he decided to fall back on something that he had had some success with in the past: writing. He submitted a series of letters to Virginia City's *Territorial Enterprise,* one of the best-known newspapers in the West, as well as to the local *Esmeralda Star.* In a letter to Orion, Sam wrote that his debts were piling up, and he insisted, "The fact is, I must have something to do, and that shortly, too."

The first letter to appear in the *Enterprise*, in April 1862, was a parody of the traditional, cliché-filled, Fourth of July political speech of the time, typically orated by the type of egotistical lecturer whom Clemens referred to as "Professor Personal Pronoun." According to Twain's official biographer, Albert Bigelow Paine, this initial letter closed by noting that it was "impossible to print his lecture in full, as the type-cases had run out of capital I's." While historians debate whether or not Clemens signed these early letters with the pen name "Josh," they agree that both newspapers did publish Clemens's early work. Sadly, no copies of the *Enterprise* or the *Star* from that era exist any longer.

The letters caught the attention of William H. Barstow, business manager of the *Enterprise*, who had become acquainted with the Clemens brothers during the gathering of the Territorial Legislature. After conferring with the *Enterprise*'s editor and part owner, Joseph Goodman, Barstow sent a letter to Clemens offering him a twenty-five-dollar-per-week salary as a staff writer for the newspaper. Some historians believe that Barstow may also have been interested in hiring Clemens because Orion had influence on the awarding of valuable printing contracts for the legislature's official documents.

Despite his reluctance to admit his failure as a miner, Clemens packed up and headed to Virginia City. He arrived in September 1862 and went to work learning how to be a newspaper reporter. Because we have no issues of the *Enterprise* prior to 1865, most of what we know of his early writing has come from scrapbooks created by the Clemens brothers, as well as from other newspapers' reprints of his work. Fortunately, these fragments of copy, from what must have been several hundred column inches, include some of his most memorable fake-news stories.

The Samuel Clemens who arrived in Virginia City was a bit rough, to say the least. Journalist and jurist C. C. Goodwin, who would serve as editor of the *Enterprise* from 1873 to 1880, later described Clemens's arrival at the newspaper like this: "A man walked in, shod in stogy shoes, wearing Kentucky jean pants, a hickory shirt, and a straw hat, all very much travel worn, and in addition had a roll of ancient blankets on one shoulder. He shrugged that shoulder, dropped the blankets, and starting from one man to another, finally drawled out, 'My name is Clemens.' This was Mark's introduction to real journalism in Nevada."

Just prior to Clemens's death, on April 22, 1910, Joseph Goodman, then living in Alameda, CA, was interviewed by the *San Francisco Examiner* and was asked to recall when he had first met his former, famous staff member:

> "Let me see—it was in 1862 that Sam Clemens came to work for us on the *Territorial Enterprise*. He was prospecting in Esmeralda County and had sent us some voluntary contributions. They struck us as so funny that we sent him word to come to Virginia City and take a job on the paper.
>
> "He came, and we put him to work reporting local affairs. Later on, we sent him to Carson [City] to report a session of the legislature, and it was from Carson that he sent us his first article signed 'Mark Twain.' He had asked me if he might sign a name to some stories apart from the regular reports of the daily proceedings in the legislature, and I had told him he might. So he wrote a humorous series of letters on what he called 'The Third House,' which described amusingly the carrying-on of a number of congenial legislators that were in the habit of gathering for a jolly social time after both houses of the legislature had adjourned overnight."

Arthur McEwen, another former staffer at the *Enterprise,* recalled that Goodman and Clemens were an unlikely duo in the beginning: "Goodman and Clemens, no men could be more unlike outwardly. The first was handsome, gallant, self-reliant but not self-conscious, vehement of speech and swift in action. . . . Clemens was sloth-like in movement, had an intolerable drawl, and punished those who offended him by long-drawn out sneering speech. But the two were alike at bottom in one thing—both were genuine, and had the quality of brain that enables one man to understand another of opposite temperament and manner. They soon became friends."

News Is Serious Business—or Not

If later accounts are to be believed (since the actual newspapers no longer exist), Clemens's self-introduction to *Enterprise* readers—his first written piece as a staff writer for the newspaper—was fairly straightforward but reflected his wit and sense of humor: "A thunderstorm made Beranger a poet, a mother's kiss made Benjamin West a painter and a salary of $15 a week makes me a journalist." This often-repeated quote, however, did not become widely circulated until after it appeared in a story in the *Dallas Morning News* on November 17, 1907, so its veracity cannot be confirmed.

One of the first-known instances of Clemens engaging in obvious exaggeration in an otherwise straight news story appeared in the *Enterprise* on October 1, 1862. In the local-news column, Clemens wrote a brief piece titled "A Gale," which included the following:

> About 7 o'clock Tuesday evening (Sept. 30) a sudden blast of wind picked up a shooting gallery, two lodging houses and a drug store from their tall wooden stilts and set them down again some ten or twelve feet back of their original location, with such a degree of roughness to jostle their insides into a sort of chaos. There were many guests in the lodging houses at the time of the accident, but it is pleasant to reflect that they seized their carpet sacks and vacated the premises with an alacrity suited to the occasion. No one hurt.

He quickly followed up that piece with his first-known, full-fledged "squib," or an entirely made-up item, a few days later. On October 4, 1862, the *Enterprise* published a short piece by Clemens titled "Petrified Man." The story told of the remains of a petrified man found in the mountains south of Gravelly Ford (which was largely known as a place on the Emigrant Trail where wagons could easily cross the Humboldt River). Clemens wrote that "every limb and feature of the stony mummy was perfect, not even excepting the left leg, which had evidently been a wooden one during the lifetime of the owner—which lifetime, by the way, came to a close about a century ago."

The petrified man, the story continued, was found in a sitting position, leaning against a rock outcropping, with "the right thumb resting against the side of the nose; the left thumb partially supported the chin, the forefinger pressing the inner corner of the left eye and drawing it partly open; the right eye was closed, and the fingers of the right hand spread apart." The specificity of Clemens's description of the man's bizarre final repose—not to mention the strange fact that the stone man had a wooden leg—practically screamed to the readers that this story was not to be believed.

He went on to write that the discovery caused such a commotion that a local judge (Clemens identified him as "Justice Sewell or Sowell") immediately visited the site of the discovery to conduct an inquest and convene a jury. The latter determined that the man had died of "protracted exposure" but that when local citizens had attempted to bury him, they had found that years of dripping limestone water had affixed him to the surrounding rocks. The judge denied a request to blast the man from the stone out of respect for the dead. Still, Clemens noted, "Everybody goes to see the stone man, as many as three hundred visited the hardened creature during the past five or six weeks."

Clemens later wrote that he had concocted the piece to mock the real Judge Sewell, a pompous politician whom Clemens apparently had had some dealings with while residing in Unionville, NV. Additionally, he said that he had wanted to spoof the many newspaper accounts at that time which were reporting the discovery of various petrified things, a trend that he dubbed "petrifaction mania."

Despite the story's obviously ludicrous elements, it appeared over the next year in dozens of newspapers around the country and in England, and many readers took it seriously. Clemens later said that he had thought that most people would read his description of the position of the stone man's hands (a variation of what the British call "cocking a snook") and would immediately recognize it as a joke. While no doubt exaggerating his suc-cess in having fooled the public—most of his readers did get the joke—he claimed: "I was too ingenious. I mixed it up rather too much; and so all that description of the attitude, as a key to the humbuggery of the article, was entirely lost, for nobody but me ever discovered and comprehended the peculiar and suggestive position of the petrified man's hands."

In her book, *Sins Against Science: The Scientific Media Hoaxes of Poe, Twain, and Others,* author Lynda Walsh Olman notes that it was not sur-prising for Twain to turn to science for many of his fake news articles. She says that science and technology had long been preoccupations of his writ-ing and business dealings, as evidenced in his admiration for the techno-logical advances displayed at the 1853 New York World's Fair, as well as in his disastrous 1880 investment in the Paige automatic typesetting machine, which he was certain would revolutionize the printing business.

The success of "Petrified Man" gave Clemens the confidence to continue developing his own unique voice in the *Enterprise,* one that occasionally relied on exaggeration, satire, farce, or prevarication. While he mostly pro-duced fairly straightforward writing for the paper, he occasionally indulged in playful and sarcastic banter with his contemporaries. For example, when his good friend and fellow *Enterprise* staffer Dan De Quille left Virginia

City in late December 1862, for a nine-month visit to see his family in Iowa, Clemens wrote a mock eulogy, "The Illustrious Departed."

In the piece, believed to be the first local column he ever concocted, Clemens wrote, "Old Dan is gone, that good old soul, we ne'er shall see him more—for some time." He continued by noting that De Quille had been worn down by his hard work as a reporter covering the local mining scene and certainly needed the rest: "His constitution suddenly warped, split and went under, and Daniel succumbed." Clemens concluded the column by expressing his hope that the 1,800-mile journey would "so restore our loved and lost to his ancient health, and energy. . . ." He added, "Dan is gone, but he departed in a blaze of glory, the likes of which hath hardly been seen upon this earth since the blameless Elijah went up in his fiery chariot."

The piece was grandiose and over the top—and just a warm-up for what was to come.

"Mark One, Mark Twain"

On February 3, 1863, Clemens's work appeared for the first time under the byline Mark Twain. The occasion was a letter to the *Enterprise* reporting on the proceedings of the Territorial Legislature session in Carson City. Using a pseudonym was a common practice; it provided the writer with an opportunity to report in a more personal way. For Clemens, it also meant having the freedom to write exactly what he thought.

But why the name Mark Twain? The true origin for Clemens's famous nom de plume has long been a bit of a mystery. Clemens, as well as close friends including Joseph Goodman, insisted that the name was borrowed from a riverboat captain, an old Clemens acquaintance who had written under that name years earlier. Goodman told the *San Francisco Examiner* in 1910 that Clemens had borrowed it from "an old Mississippi river captain named [Isaiah] Sellers who, after retiring from active service on the old-time stern-wheelers, had taken to writing the news of the river and its steamboating, and signed his stories 'Mark Twain.'" Sellers's stories allegedly appeared in several New Orleans newspapers. The name was said to have originated from a riverboat pilot's responsibility to take soundings in the Mississippi River. The pilot would call out the depth of the water while using a weighted measuring line, shouting, "Mark One, Mark Twain (for two)," etc., to indicate the river's levels. That version of the pen-name story appeared in *Mark Twain, A Biography,* published by Albert Bigelow Paine in 1912, and this was, for many years, the accepted origin story.

Later scholars, however, found no record that Captain Sellers had ever written under that pen name in any New Orleans newspaper. In 1947 Nevada historian Effie Mona Mack uncovered a different account regarding the roots of Clemens's pen name. According to her, in May 1877 George W. Cassidy, who knew Clemens in Virginia City, wrote a column in the *Eureka Daily Sentinel* in which he sought to clarify how Clemens had come up with the name Mark Twain. Cassidy, who was part owner of the *Sentinel* from 1870 until his death in 1892, and who served two terms as Nevada's representative in Congress, wrote that Clemens's riverboat story "won't work; it is too thin." He explained:

> We knew Clemens in the early days, and know exactly how he came to be dubbed "Mark Twain." John Piper's saloon, on B Street, used to be the grand rendezvous for all of the Virginia City Bohemians. Piper conducted a cash business and refused to keep any books. As a special favor, however, he would occasionally chalk down drinks to the boys on the wall back of the bar. Sam Clemens, when localizing for the Enterprise, always had an account, with the balance against him, on Piper's wall. Clemens was by no means a Coal Oil Tommy, he drank for the pure and unadulterated love of the ardent. Most of his drinking was conducted in single-handed contests, but occasionally he would invite Dan De Quille, Charley Parker, Bob Lowery or Alfred Doten, never more than one of them, however, at a time, and whenever he did his invariable parting injunction to Piper was to "mark twain," meaning two chalk marks, of course.

Upon seeing Cassidy's account, which was reprinted in the more widely circulated *Daily Alta California* newspaper, Clemens quickly fired off a letter to the *Alta* that restated the riverboat captain origin story and concluded: "This is the history of the *nom de plume* I bear."

Yet another explanation has come forward in recent years. Twain scholar Kevin Mac Donnell has argued that none of the previously proposed origin stories is correct. He has written that a more likely explanation for the name is that Clemens appropriated it from a comic sketch that had appeared in an 1861 issue of *Vanity Fair*, the most popular comic journal of his time (not to be confused with the current magazine of the same name). Mac Donnell has pointed out that one of Clemens's mentors, the lecturer and writer Artemus Ward (real name: Charles Farrar Browne), had served for a time as editor of the publication and most likely was the author of the sketch containing the name.

As Mac Donnell has indicated, Clemens would have had easy access to copies of *Vanity Fair*, which were not only sold in Carson City and Virginia City but which were also exchanged as part of a free program that was offered by the US Postal Service at that time. Newspapers and periodicals participated in the program in order to receive news stories from other parts of the country, which they often reprinted or used as filler in their own publications.

In addition, Mac Donnell has noted that one of Clemens's duties at the *Enterprise* was to review the pages of newspapers and journals from the exchange files and to cut out any items that readers might find entertaining or informative. As a result, according to Mac Donnell, Clemens may have encountered the name while reviewing papers from the exchange and then may have simply appropriated it.

In the end, we'll probably never know the true origin of the nom de plume—and that is perhaps appropriate. It is just another example of Twain's ingenuity: even today we are still attempting to sort out the truth in yet another tall tale by a master hoaxer.

FOILS AND FEUDS

Another literary device often employed by Clemens in his writing for the *Enterprise* was the use of a foil, a person whom he could mock and with whom he could feud. Indeed, real feuds with rival newspapers were common in those days. The foil could be an actual person, typically a friend or rival newspaper staffer, or could be someone he simply created for the occasion. These characters often provided a narrative tool for moving Clemens's story along. In his legislative letters, Clemens concocted "the Unreliable," who was in reality Clement T. Rice, his good friend, occasional roommate, and a journalist at a rival paper, the *Virginia Daily Union*. In response, Rice often responded in his columns by writing in a disparaging manner about a character whom he, in turn, called "the Reliable" (Clemens).

In his February 3 letter, Clemens teased the Unreliable, writing that his foil had invited himself to a party hosted by former California governor J. Neely Johnson, who had relocated to Carson City:

> About nine o'clock the Unreliable came and asked Gov. Johnson to let him stand on the porch. That creature has got more impudence than

any person I ever saw in my life. Well, he stood and flattened his nose
against the parlor window, and looked hungry and vicious—he always
looks that way—until Col. Musser [one of Carson City's founders]
arrived with some ladies, when he actually fell in their wake and came
swaggering in, looking as if he thought he had been anxiously expected.

The Unreliable appeared in all three of Clemens's letters to the *Enterprise* that were printed during the first week of February. In the latter two
letters, Clemens recounted the events surrounding the marriage of the
daughter of another Carson City founder, Abraham Curry, and he chas-
tised the Unreliable, saying: "His instincts always prompt him to go where
he is not wanted, particularly if anything of an unusual nature is on foot.
Therefore, he was present and saw those wedding ceremonies through the
parlor windows."

Similar to what he had done in writing his eulogy of Dan De Quille,
Clemens wrote a sonorous, fake obituary for the Unreliable that appeared
in the *Enterprise* on February 26, 1863. The piece began:

> He became a newspaper reporter, and crushed Truth to earth and kept
> her there, he bought and sold his own notes, and never paid his board;
> he pretended great friendship for Gillespie [Clemens's roommate at
> the time, William M. Gillespie], in order to get to sleep with him, then
> he took advantage of his bed fellow and robbed him of his glass eye
> and false teeth; of course he sold the articles, and Gillespie [who served
> as the secretary to the first constitutional convention to establish state-
> hood for Nevada] was obliged to issue more county scrip than the law
> allowed, in order to get them back again; the Unreliable broke into my
> trunk at Washoe City, and took jewelry and fine clothes and things,
> worth thousands and thousands of dollars; he was present, without
> invitation, at every party and ball and wedding which transpired in
> Carson during thirteen years.

Pushing the Limits

In mid-April 1863, Clemens, then serving as the *Enterprise*'s local editor,
contributed a brief item called "Horrible Affair," which recounted a tragic
story about a man named John Campbell, who had shot two local police-
men one night and had holed up in a Gold Hill mining tunnel. Wary of
pursuing him in the dark, officials had blocked the tunnel's entrance to trap

him until they could return the next day. Unfortunately, according to the story, a group of Native Americans (three men, a woman, and a child) had decided to shelter in the tunnel earlier that night, and when the entrance was covered with large stones, they had been overcome by the tunnel's "foul atmosphere" and had died in their sleep.

While not claiming that the story was anything more than "rumor," Clemens noted that the paper had received assurances that the story was true, and he added, "The intention of the citizens was good, but the result was most unfortunate. To shut up a murderer in a tunnel was well enough, but to leave him there all night was calculated to impair his chances for a fair trial—the principle was good, but the application was unnecessarily 'hefty.' We have given the above story for truth—we shall continue to regard it as such until it is disproven."

It turned out that portions of the story were true—Campbell had killed two police officers and had hidden in a Gold Hill tunnel—but the article appears to have been an attempt by Clemens to draw attention to the cruelty of trapping people in this way, in this instance, not only Campbell but also an innocent, albeit fictional, Native American family, in a tunnel filled with unhealthy air (as most mines were known to have had) for an entire night rather than resorting to a more humane solution, such as simply guarding the tunnel entrance and waiting for the man to emerge so that he could be brought to justice. As in many of his hoaxes, Clemens was utilizing a sensational and attention-grabbing story to encourage readers to ponder the moral or ethical implications of a certain course of action. Interestingly, in reprinting the story a few days later (a common practice at the time), the *San Francisco Herald and Mirror* noted that the *Enterprise* was "given to 'sells,'" meaning that it often published exaggerated or even fake news, and the *Herald and Mirror* wondered if this was another example.

Several months later, in late October, Clemens published one of his most famous squibs, "A Bloody Massacre near Carson." In this piece, which was widely reprinted by other newspapers throughout the country, he described the murder of a local family in particularly graphic and bloody terms. According to the story, a forty-two-year-old man named Philip Hopkins, who had lived in a log house "at the edge of the great pine forest which lies between Empire City and Dutch Nick's [east of Carson City]," had inexplicably stabbed and hacked to death his wife and nine children. Clemens wrote that Hopkins, after murdering his family and scalping his wife, had cut his own throat "from ear to ear" and then had ridden on horseback into Carson City, where he had expired promptly without speaking a word.

After describing the carnage in considerable detail, Clemens said that Hopkins had been a businessman and had owned stock in many of the best mines in Virginia City and Gold Hill. But, after San Francisco newspapers had "exposed the game of cooking dividends in order to bolster up" Comstock mining stocks, he had sold his stocks and had invested heavily in the Spring Valley Water Company of San Francisco. When it turned out that that company was also indulging in similar stock manipulations, he had gone mad and had killed his family. In conclusion, Clemens noted, the San Francisco papers had chosen to overlook the water company's misdeeds, despite the fact that the papers had covered those of the Nevada mining companies. "We hope the fearful massacre detailed above may prove the saddest result of their silence," he wrote.

Years later, Clemens said that his purpose in writing the story had been to draw attention to the inconsistencies in how some San Francisco newspapers had performed their duties as public watchdogs, and, more specifically, to punk the *Daily Evening Bulletin's* editors because their scrutiny of Virginia City's stocks had been motivated by self-interest rather than by the public interest—two of the *Bulletin's* editors had allegedly lost more than $65,000, due to Comstock silver-stock manipulations.

The graphic nature of the story generated so much negative reaction, however, that a day after it appeared in the paper, Clemens wrote a testy retraction:

> I TAKE IT BACK. The story published in the *Enterprise* reciting the slaughter of a family near Empire was all a fiction. It was understood to be such by all acquainted with the locality in which the alleged affair occurred. In the first place, Empire City and Dutch Nick's are one, and in the next there is no "great pine forest" nearer than the Sierra Nevada mountains. But it was necessary to publish the story in order to get the fact into the San Francisco papers that the Spring Valley Water Company was "cooking" dividends by borrowing money to declare them on for its stockholders. The only way you can get a fact into a San Francisco journal is to smuggle it through some great tragedy.

Clemens, however, was also growing restless about staying in Virginia City and wanted to seek new challenges elsewhere. His discontentment surfaced in his sarcastic and downright mean-spirited response to a letter to the editor sent to the *Enterprise* in April 1864. The paper regularly received letters from people living in other parts of the country, asking about living conditions, available work, climate, diseases, and other information regarding Virginia City. One such letter from "William" of Springfield, MO, said that he and several others wanted to immigrate there in the spring but wanted to make sure that the city would provide better opportunities for them. He also asked if the newspaper's staff knew a person named Joel H. Smith, who, he said owned a "considerable" mine in Nevada. In response, Clemens wrote:

> Your object in writing is to have me give you a full history of Nevada. The flattering confidence you repose in me, William, is only equalled by the modesty of your request. I could detail the history of Nevada in five hundred pages octavo, but as you have never done me any harm, I will spare you, though it will be apparent to everybody that I would be justified in taking advantage of you if I were a mind to do it. However, I will condense. Nevada was discovered many years ago by the Mormons, and was called Carson county. It only became Nevada in 1861, by act of Congress. There is a popular tradition that God Almighty created it; but when you come to see it, William, you will think differently. Do not let that discourage you, though. The country looks something like a singed cat, owing to the scarcity of shrubbery, and also resembles that animal in the respect that it has more merits than its personal appearance would seem to indicate.

Clemens proceeded to respond to each of William's questions, including one about the character of the climate:

> It has no character to speak of, William, and alas! in this respect it resembles many, ah, too many chambermaids in this wretched, wretched world. Sometimes we have the seasons in their regular order, and then again we have winter all the summer and summer all winter. Consequently, we have never yet come across an almanac that would just exactly fit this latitude. It is mighty regular about not raining, though, William. It will start in here in November and rain about four, and sometimes as much as seven days on a stretch; after that, you may loan out your umbrella for twelve months, with the serene confidence

which a Christian feels in four aces. Sometimes the winter begins in November and winds up in June; and sometimes there is a bare suspicion of winter in March and April, and summer all the balance of the year. But as a general thing, William, the climate is good, what there is of it.

Regarding what was produced in Nevada, Clemens wrote:

On our ranches here, anything can be raised that can be produced on the fertile fields of Missouri. But ranches are very scattering—as scattering, perhaps, as lawyers in heaven. Nevada, for the most part, is a barren waste of sand, embellished with melancholy sage-brush, and fenced in with snow clad mountains. But these ghastly features were the salvation of the land, William, for no rightly constituted American would have ever come here if the place had been easy of access, and none of our pioneers would have staid [*sic*] after they got here if they had not felt satisfied that they could not find a smaller chance for making a living anywhere else.

As for the presence of any deadly diseases in the state, Clemens offered, with tongue obviously in cheek:

Well, they used to die of conical balls and cold steel, mostly, but here lately erysipelas and the intoxicating bowl have got the bulge on those things. . . . We are afflicted with all the diseases incident to the same latitude in the States, I believe, with one or two added and half a dozen subtracted on account of our superior altitude. However, the doctors are about as successful here, both in killing and curing, as they are anywhere.

He concluded by noting:

Now, William, ponder this epistle well; never mind the sarcasm, here and there, and the nonsense, but reflect upon the plain facts set forth, because they are facts, and are meant to be so understood and believed. Remember me affectionately to your friends and relations, and especially to your venerable grand-mother, with whom I have not the pleasure to be acquainted—but that is of no consequence, you know. I have been in your town many a time, and all the towns of the neighboring counties—the hotel keepers will recollect me vividly. Remember me to them—I bear them no animosity. Yours, affectionately, MARK TWAIN.

GOING TOO FAR

After penning his response to William, Clemens wrote what is recognized as his most notorious and offensive effort, which historian Ronald M. James has described as "a botched hoax that inspired threats of violence and helped end [Twain's] career as a reporter with Virginia City's *Territorial Enterprise*." In the article, Clemens claimed that a Carson City women's group, which was raising money for the Sanitary Fund (the predecessor to the Red Cross that was working to help Civil War veterans), was actually using the proceeds to support a miscegenation society in the eastern United States. In Clemens's later recollection, Goodman had been out of town in May 1864 and had placed him in charge of the *Enterprise*'s editorial pages. On May 16 Clemens wrote a short piece as a joke, in which he claimed that the Sanitary Fund money was going to an organization that promoted interracial marriage (which was largely deemed to be immoral at the time). He showed the piece to De Quille, and they both agreed that it was a bit too raw and controversial to be used in the newspaper.

Writing in the winter 2021 *Nevada Historical Society Quarterly*, James explained that Clemens's intention in writing the piece was to satirize an 1863 anti-Abraham Lincoln pamphlet, *Miscegenation: The Theory of the Blending of the Races, Applied to the American White Man and Negro*, which was then making the rounds. While pointing out that Clemens may not have intended to publish the article, James questioned why he had written it in the first place, noting, "Twain only succeeded in being cruel and political in the basest sense of the word."

Clemens, who later insisted that he had been drunk when he had written the piece, said that the story had found its way into print when a press foreman, who had been collecting stories to typeset for the next day's newspaper, had picked up the miscegenation article by mistake. He had placed it in the next day's paper, the May 17 edition.

The story (a complete copy of which no longer exists) generated immediate outrage, and, on May 19, four women on the Carson City Sanitary Ball Committee sent a letter to the *Enterprise* protesting the editorial and demanding that the author admit to being a liar. By then, Goodman had returned to his editorial duties. His initial response was to ignore the letter, but he soon realized that this issue was not going to disappear.

On May 20 Clemens wrote a letter to his sister-in-law, Mollie Clemens (wife of Orion), who lived in Carson City, to apologize, explain what had happened, and request her help in quelling the growing controversy. He admitted that he was not sober when he had written the editorial and insisted that he had never intended for it to appear in the paper. He added, however, that he could not accept the humiliation that would come from admitting that he had written it while drunk and from acknowledging that he was a liar.

But the controversy would not go away and was further fanned by the rival *Virginia Daily Union*, which published the women's letter on May 21, along with a claim that the *Enterprise* had not paid a promised financial contribution to the Sanitary Fund. The *Daily Union*, which followed up on the subject for several days, called Clemens "an unmitigated liar, a poltroon and a puppy" and demanded that the *Enterprise* publish a retraction of the article.

On May 23 Clemens sent an apology to Mrs. William K. Cutler, president of the Carson City Sanitary Ball committee, and followed it up a day later with an apology in the *Enterprise,* which said, in part, "We published a rumor, the other day, that the moneys collected at the Carson Fancy Dress Ball were to be diverted from the Sanitary Fund and sent forward to aid a 'miscegenation' or some sort of Society in the East. We also stated that the rumor was a hoax. And it was—we were perfectly right. However, four ladies are offended. We cannot quarrel with ladies—the very thought of such a thing is repulsive; neither can we consent to offend them even unwittingly—without being sorry for the misfortune, and seeking their forgiveness, which is a kindness we hope they will not refuse."

The issue continued to fester despite Clemens's hope that he had resolved the matter. In a subsequent letter to Orion and Mollie, he said that he was tired of the whole affair, adding, "For Heaven's sake give me at least the peace and quiet it will afford me to know that no stumping is to be done for the unlucky Sanitary Fund." In the letter, he also mentions three persons who had allegedly issued challenges against him (which he later described as horsewhippings or duels), including William K. Cutler, husband of one of the women offended by the article. While it's unlikely that such threats were the primary reason, two days later Clemens asked his brother for two hundred dollars because he planned to leave Virginia City and relocate to San Francisco. Clemens would later embellish the story of his leaving the Queen of the Comstock by claiming that he had fled the city to avoid a duel with Cutler.

Whatever the truth—always a difficult thing to determine in matters related to Clemens—it is known that he departed Virginia City, bound for San Francisco, in the company of his friends Steve Gillis and Joe Goodman on May 29. Perhaps not surprisingly, the *Gold Hill Daily News,* another rival of the *Enterprise,* marked his departure with considerable snark:

> Among the few immortal names of the departed—that is, those who departed yesterday morning per California stage—we notice that of Mark Twain. We don't wonder. Mark Twain's beard is full of dirt, and his face is black before the people of Washoe. Giving way to the idiosyncratic eccentricities of an erratic mind, Mark has indulged in the game infernal—in short, "played hell." Shifting the locale of his tales of fiction from the Forest of Dutch Nick's to Carson City, the *dramatis personae* thereof from the Hopkins family to the fair Ladies of the Ladies Fair; and the plot thereof from murder to miscegenation—he slopped. The indignation aroused by his enormities has been too crushing to be borne by living man, though sheathed with the brass and triple cheek of Mark Twain. . . . He has vamoosed, cut slack, absquatulated; and among the pine forests of the Sierras, or amid the purlieus of the city of earthquakes, he will tarry awhile, and the office of the *Enterprise* will become purified.

Clemens would never return to live in Virginia City, although he did visit twice to lecture. After a couple of years working in San Francisco for various publications, while continuing to send regular missives to the *Enterprise,* he embarked on a visit to the Sandwich Islands (Hawaii), which ultimately led him to a long career as a renowned humorist, lecturer, and author (his first book, published in 1869, was *The Innocents Abroad,* which was about his visit to Hawaii; his second, published in 1872, was *Roughing It,* a tongue-in-cheek recounting of his time in Nevada).

A few years after his tenure at the *Enterprise,* Clemens reflected on his fake news contributions in a letter that he wrote to the paper in March 1868. In it, he noted: "To find a petrified man, or break a stranger's leg, or cave an imaginary mine, or discover some dead Indians in a Gold Hill tunnel, or massacre a family at Dutch Nick's, were feats and calamities that we never hesitated about devising when the public needed matters of thrilling interest for breakfast. The seemingly tranquil *Enterprise* office was a ghastly factory of slaughter, mutilation and general destruction in those days."

Following his short time in Virginia City, Clemens would, of course, go on to write some of the most beloved books in American literature, including *The Adventures of Huckleberry Finn, The Adventures of Tom Sawyer,* and *A Connecticut Yankee in King Arthur's Court.* On April 21, 1910, he died of a heart attack in his home in Redding, CT. He was seventy-four years old.

4

The Master

*I used to make the newspaper my notebook. . .and I thought
what a book I could write someday out of that notebook.*

~ DAN DE QUILLE (WILLIAM WRIGHT), circa 1890 ~

WHEN TWENTY-SIX-YEAR-OLD Samuel Clemens first arrived at
Virginia City's *Territorial Enterprise,* he was fortunate to have one
of its more-experienced reporters, William Wright, take him under his
wing. Wright, who wrote under the pun-worthy pen name Dan De Quille
(often spelled DeQuille), was seven years older than Clemens and had been
reporting for the paper since 1861.

In his relatively short time at the *Enterprise,* De Quille had established
a reputation for being a reliable and polished writer and was already considered one of the top mining journalists in the West. "Dan was a versatile, easy,
off-hand writer, full of quaint, original humor and as an industrious wide-
awake reporter he could pick up columns of lively and interesting items
where few could see anything at all," noted Alfred "Alf" Doten, a contemporary of both Clemens and De Quille.

Born on a farm near Fredericktown, OH, on May 9, 1829, De Quille
relocated to West Liberty, IA, with his family when he was eighteen. The
family's Quaker heritage may have influenced the writer's general demeanor,
often described as gentle and good-natured. In 1852 he married Carolyn
Coleman. He had five children with her in quick succession (two died as
infants), and he started his own farm on land adjacent to his family's holdings. Five years later, he heard the siren call of the California gold rush
and, leaving his family behind, traveled west to seek his fortune. He only
returned twice to Iowa during the next forty years—in 1862 and at the end
of his life—but he always sent money home to his wife and family.

For the next three years, De Quille prospected throughout eastern

California. Then, in 1860, he moved to Silver City to try to get in on the Comstock Lode silver and gold boom. According to Lawrence I. Berkove, who studied the writer extensively and who was largely responsible for renewed interest in his works, De Quille had begun using his pen name while still living in Iowa. Once in California, he supplemented his mining income by penning travel letters for San Francisco periodicals, such as the *Golden Era.*

JOINING THE TEAM

In 1861 Joseph Goodman and Denis McCarthy, impressed by De Quille's writing, offered him a position on the *Territorial Enterprise,* which they had recently acquired. At the *Enterprise,* De Quille excelled at covering the mining industry, reporting local news, and writing feature stories.

Goodman, in describing his employee, said that De Quille was often perceived to be quiet and unassuming but was not afraid to back up what he wrote—a trait that all successful Comstock-era journalists had to have. Goodman recalled that De Quille once wrote about a local desperado named "Farmer" Peel in a blunt manner. Some of the *Enterprise*'s print-ers, as a joke, told De Quille that Peel had stopped by the newspaper office several times, looking to confront him. Goodman said that once De Quille heard the story, he finished his work for the day and then went searching for Peel in local saloons.

Once he found him, De Quille supposedly walked up to Peel, pinned his arms, and put a stiletto knife against his throat. He said that if Peel was looking for him, they could settle any grudge on the spot. Peel's denial of any malice toward De Quille was so heartfelt that De Quille withdrew the knife and apologized for the misunderstanding. Peel reputedly later described De Quille as the only man who had ever gotten the drop on him, then treated him to a drink, and Peel insisted that there were no hard feel-ings. Goodman claimed that as a result of the episode, De Quille became so well respected and so well liked on the Comstock that he was never chal-lenged again.

By 1862 De Quille had become the *Enterprise*'s local editor, responsible for keeping tabs on the community's activities, arrests and crimes, agricul-tural news, and other happenings. Additionally, he continued to contribute sketches, travel pieces, and other features to the *Golden Era.* That year, he also started working alongside the paper's newest hire, Mark Twain (then still called by his real name, Samuel Clemens). The two became fast friends, with De Quille serving as an early mentor to the raw but obviously talented Twain.

In a place like Virginia City, where scams such as fake discoveries, "salted" mines, and mining stock manipulation were everyday occurrences, it was unsurprising that hoaxes and fake stories would come naturally to Comstock journalists like De Quille and Twain. But while Twain was honing his satirical skills at the *Enterprise* by jousting with rival newspaper editors and politicians (as well as with De Quille), and by cooking up stories about fake murders, De Quille excelled at the science-based hoax. And because of his fairly extensive knowledge of contemporary science and technology, De Quille's flights of fancy had the ring of truth.

"De Quille was the master of the art of the hoax, and no discussion of this distinctively American form can be complete without attention to his contributions," according to scholars Lawrence I. Berkove and Michael Kowalewski in their 1997 book *Updating the Literary West.* "Some of his hoaxes consisted of broad and obvious humor, as when he engaged his roommate Mark Twain in mock duels of calumny in the columns of the *Enterprise,* where each would enormously but hilariously magnify into miracles of disaster minor injuries the other sustained. Some of his hoaxes rank with the best ever devised and are American classics."

University of Nevada professor Lynda Walsh Olman writes that De Quille's scientific fakery "was deeply conditioned by both Poe's and Twain's hoaxes but was ultimately a different project from theirs." She says that Poe wrote for a different audience—eastern city dwellers—while both Twain and De Quille were writing for western pioneers, who were independent in thought and often skeptical of outsiders. She says that De Quille, in particular, could relate to his readers, who were "stubborn old comstockers," having been a miner himself. He also enjoyed science, geology, and other scientific subject matter (unlike Twain), and his personal papers contain dozens of clippings focused on the scientific side of mining, as well as on some "pseudoscientific" subjects, such as extrasensory perception, thought transference, and other less-mainstream scientific ideas.

Walsh Olman notes that at least part of De Quille's motivation for writing his hoaxes was because he was so invested in Nevada's success. He focused all of his stories on the state because, she writes, "He knew that hoaxes created new realities for readers, both western and eastern. The hoaxes, along with De Quille's other stories, served to create a larger-than-life legend of Nevada as a scientific wonderland and Nevadans as stout-hearted individualists who did not shy away from the most bizarre of discoveries."

The "Quaints"

One of De Quille's earliest fake-news stories was "A Silver Man," published in the *Golden Era* in February 1865. In the feature, which many historians believe was inspired by Mark Twain's similarly named hoax story "The Petrified Man," De Quille described the discovery of an unusual, petrified man's body in a cave southeast of Mono Lake. Incorporating his scientific knowledge, De Quille wrote that the man, most likely a Native American, became trapped in the cave and starved to death. Over time, allegedly, various minerals in the ground essentially fused with the body. The result of this quasi-scientific transmutation was a corpse made of silver and other minerals.

Another of De Quille's "quaints," one of his best known, was a story about a man who invented "solar armor," which was designed to protect the wearer from the brutal desert sun. Appearing in the *Territorial Enterprise* in July 1874, the story was reprinted in *Scientific American,* London's *Daily Telegraph,* and publications around the world. The piece described the "sad fate" of Jonathan Newhouse, an inventor who had developed an apparatus that could protect a person from the sun's worst heat. De Quille described the armor as:

> A long, close-fitting jacket made of common sponge and a cap or hood of the same material; both jacket and hood being about an inch in thickness. Before starting across the desert this armor was to be saturated with water. Under the right arm was suspended an India rubber sack filled with water and having a small gutta percha tube leading to the top of the hood. In order to keep the armor moist, all that was necessary to be done by the traveler, as he progressed over the burning sands, was to press the sack occasionally, when a small quantity of water would be forced up and thoroughly saturate the hood and the jacket below it.

De Quille said that Newhouse went down to Death Valley with several companions, leaving them behind to wait while he made a two-day trek alone through that hot and dry place to test his invention. A day after he had departed, however, a Native American who could speak only a few words of

English came to the camp where Newhouse's associates were awaiting his return. The Native American was agitated about something but unable to communicate with the men, so he wanted them to follow him.

"At the distance of about twenty miles out into the desert the Indian pointed to a human figure seated against a rock," De Quille continued. "Approaching they found it to be Newhouse still in his armor. He was dead and frozen stiff. His beard was covered with frost and—though the noonday sun poured down its fiercest rays—an icicle over a foot in length hung from his nose. There he had perished miserably, because his armor had worked but too well, and because it was laced up behind where he could not reach the fastenings."

After the story had circulated, De Quille received word that one newspaper, the *Daily Telegraph* in London, was skeptical. In response, he doubled down on his hoax, explaining in a second article, published about a month later, that the justice of the peace and coroner of Salt Wells, NV, near where Newhouse was found, had conducted an inquest. These authorities had determined that the solar armor had not relied on plain water as a coolant but had instead depended on a concoction of unknown chemicals developed by the inventor. The inquest report, as De Quille fabricated it, said:

> We find that the name of the deceased was Jonathan Newhouse, a native of Knox County, Ohio, aged 47 years, and we further find that deceased came to his death in Death Valley, Inyo County, California, on the 27th day of June, A.D. 1874, by being frozen in a sort of coat of sponge called a "solar armor," of which he was the inventor and in which he was tightly laced at his own request, said "solar armor" being moistened with some frigorific mixture, with the precise nature of which we are unacquainted.

Another early example of De Quille's fake-news efforts was his famous "Traveling Stones" of Pahranagat piece, published in the *Enterprise* on October 26, 1867. In this relatively brief item, De Quille wrote that some years earlier, a prospector wandering in the eastern Nevada Pahranagat Range had discovered perfectly round stones, "being of an irony nature," with a curious property: "When scattered about on the floor, on a table, or other level surface, within two or three feet of each other, they immediately began traveling toward a common center, and then huddled up in a bunch like a lot of eggs in a nest."

The stones would not move about, however, if separated by more than four or five feet. The miner claimed that he had found the miraculous stones in a rocky plain in eastern Nevada that contained a number of small basins. The traveling stones were clustered at the bottom of these basins, which measured from a few feet to two or three rods (roughly eleven to fifteen feet) in diameter, and they seemed to be made of lodestone or magnetic iron ore.

While the story didn't generate much reaction initially, it eventually spread far and wide via the US postal delivery's free newspaper exchange and began to appear in publications throughout the world. The *Enterprise* started receiving dozens of letters. Wells Drury, who worked alongside De Quille for many years, later wrote that when the tale reached Germany, it "caused a furor among a select set of men who were dabbling in the study of electro-magnetic currents." Their secretary wrote to De Quille, demanding further details. In vain, he disclaimed the verity of his skit. His denial was treated as an unprofessional attempt to keep his brother scientists ignorant of the truth concerning natural laws, the effects of which, these scientists were convinced, had been first observed and recorded by "'Herr Dan De Quille, the eminent physicist of Virginia-stadt [*sic*], Nevada.'" Showman P. T. Barnum reportedly read about the traveling nuggets and offered De Quille $10,000 if he would go on tour with his circus (De Quille politely declined).

On March 31, 1872, De Quille, who had tired of responding to the letters and requests for samples of the rocks, sought to dump the matter onto his good friend Mark Twain. Writing in the *Enterprise*, De Quille said:

> About six years ago an account of certain curious rolling stones was published in the *Enterprise*. The item has been going the rounds ever since without any one being able to suggest any plan by which money might be made out of them. A request has recently come to the local postmaster for five pounds of the stones. . . . We have none of said rolling stones in this city at present but would refer our Colorado speculator to Mark Twain, who probably has still on hand fifteen or twenty bushels of assorted sizes.

Another seven years later, De Quille again tried to put the story to rest by coming clean:

> In an idle moment, some fifteen years ago, this deponent concocted

and wrote an item entitled "Traveling Stones." The stones were said to have been brought from the Pahranagat country, where they were found in shallow basins in the rock. They were round, and ranged in size from those no bigger than a buckshot up to such as were the size of a ten-pin ball. They were evidently largely composed of magnetic iron ore, and when spread out on the floor or other level surface would all run and huddle together like a covey of quail, though when one was removed too far from its mates it could not get back.

The story of the little traveling stones seemed to supply a want that had long been felt—to fit exactly and fill a certain vacant nook in the minds of men—and they traveled through all the newspapers of the world. This we did not so much mind, nor were we much worried by letters of inquiry at first, but it has now been some years since we ceased to enjoy them. First and last, we must have had bushels of letters asking about these stones. Letter after letter have we opened from foreign parts in the expectation of hearing something to our advantage—that half a million had been left us somewhere or that somebody was anxious to pay us four bits a column for sketches about the mountains and mines—and have only found some other man wanting to know all about those traveling stones.

So it has gone on all these fifteen years. Our last is from Tiffin, Ohio, dated Nov.3, and received yesterday. His name is Haines, and he wants to know all about those stones, could he obtain several and how? Not long since we had a letter from a man in one of the New England States who informed us that there was big money in the traveling stones. We were to send him a carload, when he would exhibit and sell them, dividing the spoils with us. We have stood this thing about fifteen years, and it is becoming a little monotonous. We are now growing old, and we want peace. We desire to throw up the sponge and acknowledge the corn; therefore we solemnly affirm that we never saw or heard of any such diabolical cobbles as the traveling stones of Pahranagat—though we still think there ought to be something of the kind somewhere in the world. If this candid confession shall carry a pang to the heart of any true believer we shall be glad of it, as the true believers have panged it to us, right and left, quite long enough.

Despite his experiences with the traveling stones, De Quille wasn't quite done with hoaxes involving rocks. In the October 19, 1871, edition of the *Enterprise,* he wrote about "Ringing Rocks and Singing Stones." In this article, De Quille noted that stories had been circulating about the "ringing rocks" found in Pennsylvania (they are, in fact, not a hoax—there are stones in Bucks County, PA, that ring musically when struck; the site is now a county park). But Pennsylvania, apparently, did not have a monopoly on such marvels. De Quille also claimed that there was a hill near Pyramid Lake in Nevada, in what he called the Truckee Mining District, that had similar properties:

> It was first observed by the prospectors who discovered the district and who had pitched their camp at the foot of the hill. For several nights they were puzzled and not a little startled by a peculiar, low musical tinkling which seemed to float upon the breeze, coming and going like the notes of an aeolian harp. This occurring regularly every evening, when all was quiet, the miners set out to solve the mystery, and soon found that the sound they had heard proceeded from small stones which formed a sort of drift reaching from the base of the hill to near its summit.
>
> These stones gave out a constant tinkling sound, and their myriads of tinklings mingling together produced a musical murmur of considerable volume. The stones emitting these sounds were described as containing much iron, and some supposed that the musical tinklings were produced by magnetic action, while others thought the whole drift of stones might be slowly working down the hill, and that the sounds were caused by the attraction of the fragments composing the mass.

While this story also circulated around the country, there is no record that De Quille received letters demanding that he send samples of the singing stones.

A few years later, De Quille again filed a fake-news story that was widely distributed. This time the story involved a new species of aquatic creature, which he called the Eucalyptus. In the December 1, 1874, issue of the *Enterprise,* he wrote that the Eucalyptus, while unknown on the Atlantic Coast, was "somewhat familiar to persons residing on the Pacific Coast." He added that the creatures were currently being exhibited at Woodward's Gardens in San Francisco—site of a popular amusement park, zoo, museum, and aquarium—in the city's Mission District.

De Quille described the animals as being about twelve feet long and covered with short, black fur on their back and light, brown fur on their sides and stomach. He said the creatures were generally gentle and docile but had powerful jaws and, most interesting of all, a spine that "terminates in a fork, each branch of which extends like a tail and is some five feet in length. The vertebral bones continue through these tails, which have on their outer sides a broad, falcated membrane, along the outer edge of which, on each tail or wing are three strong hooks, similar to those seen on the wings of a bat."

One of De Quille's most widely circulated fake features appeared in the *Enterprise* on February 19, 1876. Titled "Eyeless Fish That Live in Hot Water," this tall tale claimed that miners working deep in the Hale and Norcross Mine in Virginia City had reported finding bloodred, eyeless fish swimming in the hot water found in the depths of the mines. They measured three or four inches in size and thrived in scalding, hot water.

"When the fish were taken out of the hot water in which they were found, and placed in a bucket of cold water, for the purpose of being brought to the surface, they died almost instantly. The cold water at once chilled their life blood," he wrote. "In appearance these subterranean members of the finny tribe somewhat resemble gold fish. They seem lively and sportive enough while in their native hot water, notwithstanding the fact they have no eyes nor even the rudiments of eyes."

To sell his hoax, he concluded by noting that eyeless fish are often found in lakes in large caves, while asserting that this was the first time that any type of fish had been discovered that could survive in water with such hot temperatures.

Like Twain, De Quille occasionally used hoaxes as a way to make a point about something else. To draw attention to the many misdeeds and scams being perpetrated by some mining stockbrokers and mine owners and operators, he once concocted a fake mining company, the "Pewterinctum Mining Company," and wrote a handful of satirical reports about its odious activities for the *Golden Era* and for a short-lived Comstock weekly, the *Virginia City Occidental.* For the latter, he devised a fake help-wanted brief that said:

Wanted.—A Gentleman to fill the position of Superintendent of the Pewterinctum mine. No person need apply who has not the following qualifications: A fast horse, a fast buggy and another fast horse; a heavy gold watch with a heavy gold chain, and a fine diamond pin; must have at least three fast women, a taste for liquors and some knowledge of poker; also, must have sympathy for working miners, and must be in favor of reducing their wages. A permanent situation will be given to any person having the above qualifications.

By the mid-1860s, De Quille had spun many a tale in his forty years with the *Enterprise* and had freelanced for a variety of other publications. But he had also become an alcoholic. Unfortunately, heavy drinking was a common activity for reporters during this era. As Lawrence I. Berkove has noted, nearly every Comstock journalist had to have a high tolerance for alcohol because saloons were where they found the news, established relationships, and spent their downtime.

De Quille increasingly became too inebriated to do his job on some days. Fellow journalist Alfred Doten, who maintained daily diaries of his own activities for more than fifty years, wrote in his journals of several occasions when he had to fill in for De Quille, who had become "too demoralized" to come to work. In 1872 Goodman fired De Quille, whom he often described as one of his closest friends, because of his excessive drinking. He rehired him again a few days later, but it would not be the only time that Goodman would let De Quille go—each subsequent time for longer periods—just to bring him back later.

Big Bonanza

In 1874 Goodman decided to sell the *Enterprise* to William Sharon. De Quille continued reporting for the paper but also began working on a pair of writing projects that he hoped would bring him the same kind of success that Twain had enjoyed with *Roughing It,* a book he had published in 1872. One of the projects was to be an extensive history of the Comstock and of Virginia City, while the other was to be a collection of his sketches and other literary works. He asked Twain for advice on the projects, and the latter encouraged him to combine them into one single book, which he partially did in his first book, *The History of the Big Bonanza.* In 1875 De Quille accepted Twain's invitation to stay at the latter's home in Hartford, CT, for several months to complete this book, and Twain's publishing company released it in 1876. Unfortunately, *Big Bonanza* was not a commercial success, and De Quille never found the time or energy to develop his second book, which would have been a more-literary collection of sketches not incorporated into *The History of the Big Bonanza,* including several of his hoaxes. In 1889 De Quille did publish *A History of the Comstock Silver Lode & Mines,* which was more of a promotional vehicle for fading Virginia City, with chapters devoted not only to Virginia City's colorful history but also to local attractions in surrounding communities.

The disappointing performance of *Big Bonanza* caused De Quille's once-close relationship with Twain to end, and it also pushed De Quille back into heavy drinking. In 1877 he was admitted to the County Hospital in Virginia City to help him get sober (at least for a while). Following his release, he apparently found ways to better manage his addiction for stretches of time (although he was again fired by the *Enterprise* in 1885 and didn't return for two years) and, according to Berkove, "began writing more fiction and humor [pieces] and placing them wherever he could." In addition to writing for the *Enterprise,* De Quille published articles regularly in San Francisco newspapers and in publications including *The Sacramento Bee,* the *Carson Daily Appeal, The New York Times,* the *Chicago Tribune, The Salt Lake Tribune, Overland Monthly, Cosmopolitan,* and dozens of others.

By 1897 the years of drinking finally began to affect his health seriously, and De Quille was, as Alfred Doten described him when he encountered him that year:

> [so] terribly broken down with rheumatism and used up generally, that he cannot live long anyway—Is racked with it from shoulders to knees, back humped up double and is merely animated skin and bone, almost helpless—can only walk about the house a little, grasping cane with both hands—has not been able to walk down from his residence on A st, Va, to C st & back for nearly or quite 2 yrs—looks to be 90 years old, yet was 68 on the 9th of May last—2 months & 10 days older than I am—Promised to write to me when he gets home—Poor dear old boy Dan—my most genial companion in our early Comstock reportorial days, good bye, and I think forever personally on this earth.

In 1897 De Quille decided to move back to West Liberty, IA, where he would spend the rest of his days, and he planned to travel there from Virginia City with his wife and daughter in July. During his final years, De Quille had become nearly destitute. After learning of De Quille's financial state and hearing of his travel plans, mining millionaire John Mackay—a friend who was also part owner of the *Enterprise*—immediately provided the writer with a pension of sixty dollars per week, ordered him fitted with two new suits, and provided an escort to travel with De Quille and his family to Iowa.

A month earlier, Carson City's *Silver State* newspaper had noted, "William Wright, known to the people of Nevada as Dan De Quille, wife and daughter expect to move to Iowa before long. Dan has been a resident of Nevada so long that the smell of sagebrush will cling to him wherever he goes. His pen and brain have helped to make Nevada's history and he will take with him to his new home the best wishes of every true Nevadan."

On March 16, 1898, after contracting the flu during an epidemic, De Quille died in his sleep in his daughter's home in West Liberty.

In the aftermath of De Quille's death, many of his old Comstock friends wrote glowing tributes, including Judge C. C. Goodwin, who said that his decades of work were "never equaled on a newspaper by any one man." He described him as "the old friend that was always true, always quaint, always genial; the man who did not know his own power."

In a similar vein, longtime Comstock editor Wells Drury later wrote, "Of all the men I knew on the Comstock I consider William Wright—Dan De Quille—the most thoroughly characteristic of the camp and its inhabitants." Drury described him as without peer when it came to understanding and writing about the Comstock mining industry, but he added:

> It must not be thought, however, that Dan could write nothing but mining items. He had a fund of quaint humor, and when his attention was not distracted by quartz or placers, produced some of the most readable sketches written in the West. . . . From filmy threads of unreality he evolved postulates and spun theories that startled scientists and set the Barnums of the country by the ears.

Several years after De Quille's death, Joseph Goodman reflected on how De Quille and Twain were already being viewed by history: "Isn't it so singular that Mark Twain should live and Dan De Quille fade out? If anyone had asked me in 1863 which was to be an immortal name, I should unhesitatingly have said Dan De Quille. They had about equal talent and sense of humor, but the difference was the way in which they used their gifts. One shrank from the world; the other braved it, and it recognized his audacity."

5

The Liar

It requires inventive genius to pick up local news here now.
The scribe has to trust to his imagination for facts and to
his memory for things which never occurred.

~ JAMES W. E. "LYING JIM" TOWNSEND ~

IN AN ERA when fabricating news was not all that unusual, a person would have to have been a first-class prevaricator to have earned the nickname "Lying Jim." That was, in fact, the case for James William Emery Townsend, known as "Lying Jim" for most of his career. Townsend was so renowned for being a fabulist that fellow newspaperman Wells Drury described him as "the most original writer and versatile liar that the west coast, or any coast, ever produced." That assessment was echoed by Lawrence Berkove and Michael Kowalewski, who described him in 1997's *Updating the Literary West* as "one of the most talented and notorious liars of the Comstock, no small accomplishment."

In 1899 journalist Alfred Doten depicted Townsend as "an original genius, always loaded to the muzzle with exuberant, mirthful witticisms, ready to be turned loose on any occasion. It's simply his genial, festive nature, and he can't help it. No more kindly dispositioned, generous-hearted man lives, sympathizing liberally with weaker and more suffering humanity, and always willing to divide his last dollar, if he has one, with a friend in need."

Given Townsend's propensity for tall tales, he no doubt was amused when Virginia City's *Virginia Chronicle* published a tongue-in-cheek summary of his life in 1882, which claimed: "We learn that he was born in Patagonia, his mother, a noble English lady, having been cast ashore after the wreck of her husband's yacht, in which they were making a pleasure trip around the globe. She was the only person saved. After the birth of her son. . .she was killed and eaten."

In the so-called biography, Townsend somehow managed to survive being eaten for the next twelve years, then escaped on a log, paddled through the Strait of Magellan with his bare hands, and was finally picked up by a whaler, who dropped him off in New Bedford, Massachusetts. At the age of eighteen, he became a Methodist minister and preached around the region, before spreading the gospel for twenty years in the Sandwich Islands (Hawaii), according to the biography. He then turned his back on religion, opened a saloon in New York, and made a fortune before deciding to become a journalist (and, naturally, winding up poor again). He gained his nickname "Lying Jim," allegedly, because he was once afflicted with a disease that compelled him to remain on his back for months.

"Some of his friends who are of a mathematical turn have ascertained from data furnished them by Mr. Townsend in various conversations the remarkable fact that he is 384 years old," the fake biography concluded.

The Real Lyin' Jim

Townsend's real story, however, is no less fascinating. He was born in Portsmouth, NH, on August 4, 1838, and his father was a merchant sailor. At the age of fourteen, Jim apprenticed with a local printer and quickly mastered the trade. His sole, actual biographers, Richard A. Dwyer and Richard E. Lingenfelter—who published *Lying on the Eastern Slope: James Townsend's Comic Journalism on the Mining Frontier*—report that Townsend decided to look for better prospects somewhere else, following the national financial downturn caused by the Panic of 1857. So, he signed on with a sailing ship, but whether he traveled directly to the West Coast or spent time first in some other places remains a mystery.

By 1859 he was in San Francisco and went looking for work in the print room of the *Golden Era*. Although he was just twenty-one, the confident Townsend claimed to be forty-six and to have vast experience as a typesetter. Despite his youth, he was hired and began setting type and writing occasional pieces, working alongside other young journalists who would go on to success in the field, including Bret Harte, Joseph Goodman, and Denis McCarthy, who were all in their early twenties. Goodman and McCarthy, indeed, would soon team up to purchase the *Territorial Enterprise*.

Townsend continued working as a typesetter and occasional writer in San Francisco for the next year, including doing a short stint at another San Francisco news and literary newspaper, the *Evening Mirror*. In fall 1862 he relocated to Virginia City, joining the staff of the *Enterprise,* now owned by his former coworkers, Goodman and McCarthy. Among the newspaper's reporters and editors at the time of Townsend's arrival were Samuel Clemens and Dan De Quille. Townsend befriended both and, according to Dwyer and Lingenfelter, "engaged in many bull session exchanges of yarns and witticisms that whetted and tempered the talents peculiar to each." He also established a reputation for being able to put away large quantities of whiskey—something he would continue to do for most of his life and to his eventual detriment—and for spinning the most inventive lies.

Townsend is said to have had an outsized influence on his coworkers. His propensity for telling tall tales was said to be the inspiration for the character "Truthful James" in one of western writer Bret Harte's most famous poems, "Plain Language from Truthful James." Some critics have written that Townsend may have been the person who first told Clemens the tale of the jumping frog, which the latter adapted, under his Mark Twain byline, as "The Celebrated Jumping Frog of Calaveras County" in 1865. The story had apparently circulated in mining camps for many years, so Townsend is not likely to have been the original teller, and Clemens readily acknowledged that it was a story he had heard before and was merely sharing in his own inimitable voice.

After about a year and a half at the *Enterprise*, Townsend jumped to the rival *Virginia City Daily Union*. He also found time to get married and may have had a daughter, although the marriage lasted only about six months. By late 1864 Townsend had settled in Grass Valley, CA, where he and a partner published a pro-Lincoln newspaper—at least until Townsend, without telling his partner, attempted to switch sides at the last minute (for money) and to support Lincoln's opponent. Caught red-handed, he agreed to leave the community immediately and promised never to return.

Townsend then moved back to San Francisco, where he obtained work again as a typesetter, initially at the *San Francisco Daily Times* and later at the *Alta California* newspaper. From about 1870 to 1880, he bounced around a number of communities in Northern California and Nevada, including Antioch, CA (where he cofounded the weekly *Antioch Ledger*), Sacramento, San Francisco (again), Aurora, NV, and the Columbus Salt Marsh in Nevada. In the last of these, he and several partners established the *Borax Miner*, which they operated for several years.

In June 1880 the forty-two-year-old Townsend relocated to the mining town of Lundy, CA, located near the border of California and Nevada. Within a short time, he was typesetting and writing for the local paper, the *Homer Mining Index,* which celebrated his arrival with a brief item that said: "A queer old stick is Jim with as many kinks in his mental make-up as a piece of mountain mahogany, and as jolly a dog as ever 'proved a galley.' 'A fellow of infinite jest' is this stray old print—one of your good Western talkers—whose stories combine the flavor of the mining camp and the *bonhomie* of the Bohemian over his beer."

Townsend, who was renowned for doing much of his writing on the galleys (he did not always work from a written manuscript but often composed while setting the type), began writing short quips for the paper's local columns, which were soon picked up by dozens of newspapers in Nevada and Northern California and which were often simply called "Townsendisms." Among his witticisms:

> Mill Creek is so crooked in one place that it is difficult to cross it. We waded it half a dozen times the other day and came out on the same side every time.

> The waters of Mono Lake are so buoyant that the bottom has to be bolted down, and boys paddle about on granite boulders.

> When thieves fall out honest men get their dues. But when honest men fall out lawyers get their fees.

> The editor of the *Pioche Record* says, "Mrs. Page's milk is delicious." We shall soon hear that her husband has weaned him with a club. He knows too much.

> A woman in Fresno had a cross-eyed baby the other day. There is a cross-eyed neighbor. Strained relations now exist between two men who were once chums.

> Somebody says that up in the Klondike "a miner often spends $30 in one night." Considering that the nights are about six months long, it is a cheap jag.

In late 1880, Townsend, who had constructed and was operating an arrastra (a primitive mill used for grinding and pulverizing ore), formally joined the staff of the *Index* and soon contributed more quips and humorous local items. The community, however, soon experienced the danger of having been built in a steep canyon at nearly eight thousand feet of elevation. In the winter of 1880–1881, fierce winds whipped off the mountains, slamming into the flimsy wooden structures of Lundy. Townsend described it like this:

"I lived in a solid log cabin built against a granite ledge, and yet the wind is so strong that our habitation danced a jig every time a gust came down the canyon, and now we have been blown across several lots, and our house threatens to trot into the lake."

A few days later, he wrote about the demise of a local hotel: "About 7 o'clock a fierce gust came down Main Street, and, taking the new hotel 'broadside on,' slid it from its underpinning and deposited it in the adjoining lot, leaving a double twist in the structure which could make a blind man cross-eyed to contemplate."

Despite the challenging environmental conditions—heavy snow soon followed the terrible winds—Townsend and a partner, a former Virginia City printer named Ed Everett, bought the *Index*. Soon Townsend focused his sharp wit on the local court, which Judge Henry P. Medlicott presided over. In one article, Townsend mocked charcoal drawings of the jurist that graced the walls of a lodging house which also served as the court, noting: "The sketcher shows his wonderful skill in nasal architecture, and builds a proboscis which is readily recognized. It looks something like a cross between a step-ladder and the scoop of a steam-paddy. A syringe is being applied to the starboard orifice of this monstrous nose, and somebody in the background is apparently working it for the purpose of sluicing out his Honor's head—a negative hint that the fountain of justice should be clear."

While Townsend and Everett (who would eventually sell his share to Townsend) produced a lively newspaper, they soon faced the reality that the mining town was not destined for longevity. By late 1881 the local economy was in the dumps, and Townsend himself had packed up and departed, selling his stake in the paper to veteran journalist John Ginn. After wandering through the Mother Lode area for several months, he landed in Reno, then the fastest growing town in Nevada, and the *Reno Evening Gazette* hired him to write local columns emphasizing news associated with the passengers who disembarked from the daily train.

His daily articles were more or less factual but had an edge, such as in this eyebrow-raising piece:

A ponderously fleshy woman boarded the train between Reno and Winnemucca yesterday, and when Ben Sargent, the slim and angular conductor, went to collect fare, she wanted to palm off a lot of brass jewelry as collateral for her ride. Ben said that wouldn't pay the company, and declined to receive the plunder. At Lovelock's, he tried to put

her off, but she wouldn't be dumped into the Great American Desert
without protest. The result was a most interesting scrimmage between
a very slim conductor and a very fat train-jumper.

Townsend spent the next three years writing for the Reno newspaper
while taking seasonal breaks to travel to Bodie, CA, and other parts of the
eastern Sierra Nevada. In 1885 he returned to Virginia City, where he continued to be a popular figure who was often featured in the local papers. He
worked for a time at the *Territorial Enterprise,* put away enough money to
purchase the *Carson Daily Index* in Nevada's capital city (then sold the paper
a mere three months later), and returned to Lundy in the fall of 1888.

Truth Be Damned

The community that Townsend returned to was moribund. Lundy was
nearly abandoned, so George Washington Butterfield—co-owner of the
company that controlled Lundy's mines—hired Townsend to help bring
the town back to life by falsely promoting the area mines as thriving and
filled with potential. To that end, Townsend wrote weekly mining reports
that were filled to the brim with superlatives about the mining operations
and which were jam-packed with optimistic (and vague) assessments. He
did not allow himself to be constrained by the scarcity of genuine news, so
he freely inserted fantastical, fake stories—some of his best—into the mix,
including one about a strange fish-creature allegedly sighted at Mono Lake:

> It has been universally believed that no creature of any kind can exist in
> the waters of Mono Lake; but Judge Mattly explodes this notion. Last
> Saturday he saw a strange creature flopping about in the shallow water
> near the shore. The thing seemed to open and shut like a spy-glass; at
> its longest it was about six feet in length and two feet in diameter. It
> resembled an enormous leech more than anything else, and apparently
> propelled itself by drawing in air and forcing it behind. When inflated
> it was egg-shaped and sat upon the water like a bell-buoy. No flipper
> or fins of any description were visible, nor anything that resembled a
> mouth. The orifices through which it evidently inhaled air could not be
> seen. The Judge described it as a disgusting mass of green pulp.

Another of his hoaxes, published in 1894, spotlighted a rather long-
lived goose:

A wild goose has been captured west of the Utah line. Attached to the bird's leg was a very thin piece of brass, an inch long and half as wide. On this is punched with a pointed instrument, "Fremont Party, September, 1846, B. B. J." It is presumed that the initials are those of Colonel B. B. Jackson, who was a member of Fremont's exploring expedition when it passed through the region nearly fifty years ago. The venerable colonel is living somewhere in Sonoma County, California, and has been informed of the capture. If he remembers having turned a tagged goose loose in 1846 the bird will be presented to the California Pioneer Society.

In one of his yarns with a more scientific bent, Townsend reported seeing strange lights on the slope above Lundy Lake, which, he wrote, caused boulders to begin to vibrate and move about. Somewhat similar to De Quille's "Traveling Stones" of Pahranagat piece, Townsend's hoax claimed:

On the slope of Mount Gilcrest above the lake opposite Lundy, a strange light was observed one evening recently. The Index man and a companion crossed the lake and ascended to the place where the light was seen, when they witnessed a group of granite boulders, some of them weighing many tons, all trembling violently, as if afflicted with severe ague, while the phosphorescent flashes emitted by them imparted an uncanny effulgence to surrounding objects. A hundred tons of granite boulders shivering like a Shaker prayer meeting and illuminated by a ghost-fire would puzzle anybody.

Next morning they returned to the spot, and found the boulders silent and inert, and looking as innocent as any other blocks of granite, but there was abundant evidence that they had been in motion, perhaps at long intervals for ages. They had each ground out an egg-shaped hollow in the bedrock, the only way in every instance being from north to south, and varying in depth from two feet to nine or ten. In the center of the group is a mass of magnetic iron ore. What influence this magnetic mass has upon the surrounding boulders is inexplicable at present, but it may be that by some freak of nature it becomes a storage battery, and when supercharged with the accumulations of years, alternately attracts and repels the adjacent boulders, thus giving them the ague, as it were.

Writing about Townsend years later, Wells Drury claimed, "To read his paper you would think that it was published in a city of ten thousand inhabitants. He had a mayor and a city council, whose proceedings he reported once a week, although they never existed, and enlivened his columns with killings, law suits, murder trials and railroad accidents, and a thousand incidents of daily life in a humming, growing town—every last one of which he coined out of his own active brain."

Unfortunately for Townsend, the mining scam concocted by Butterfield was uncovered when the latter was sued by unhappy investors in England. Butterfield had created a holding company, West May Lundy Company Ltd., in which he had attempted to sell $4.5 million in ownership shares for some twenty-three mines. The scheme quickly unraveled after a San Francisco newspaper, which knew the true value of Lundy's mines, called out the entire enterprise as a fraud. The story was shared in England, where Butterfield had just unloaded about $12,000 in stock. Butterfield tried to defend his enterprise as legitimate but lost in the end.

To protect his own sullied reputation, Townsend, who had been forced to reveal the truth during a legal deposition, insisted that the *Index* was independent and doubled down on his claim in an item in the paper: "[The *Index*] has never seen the color of any other man's money except it was honestly earned. He who makes an assertion to the contrary is a venomous liar and loves malicious lying as a dog loves vomit."

Fortunately for Townsend, who was now committed to publishing the *Index* without a hidden underwriter, the mines reopened the following year, which provided a glimmer of life to the community and the paper. The mining output, however, wasn't particularly outstanding, and, according to Dwyer and Lingenfelter, Townsend was forced to trade subscriptions and advertising for cords of firewood, chickens, or just about anything else he needed to survive. He also increasingly sought escape from his troubles in alcohol and, now in his mid-fifties, was starting to experience various health ailments, including arthritis and rheumatism.

By 1895 he was no longer able to produce the newspaper, and so he suspended operations. He relocated to another eastern California mining town that was also in decline, Bodie, where, amazingly, he began yet another newspaper, *The Mining Index*. He published this newspaper weekly and, despite having to hire helpers to get it out, made just enough money to keep it operating for the next few years.

In his diaries, journalist Alfred Doten wrote of encountering his old drinking pal in Carson City on Sunday, June 14, 1896: "At evening train I met Jim Townsend just from Bodie, bound for San F [Francisco]—very rheumatic but jolly as usual—Says he was born Aug 4, 1823."

Despite his failing health, Townsend continued to produce lively (and often exaggerated) copy that other publications picked up and reprinted. For example, the March 27, 1897, edition of the *Elko Independent* shared a short article titled "The Mono Lake Volcanoes," which claimed:

> One of the obsidian cones a few miles south of Mono Lake is smoking and fuming furiously, and at night a red flow is perceptible at the summit. There are three of these cones, all being dormant volcanoes with deep craters. The subterranean times are not yet extinct, and are liable to break out again any day. As the age of the world is measured, it is not a great while since the whole three were spouting lava and ashes and frightening the monster reptiles which then swarmed in the surrounding waters.

The item had an unusual postscript that perhaps clued readers into considering the source when reading it: "The above is authenticated by no less an authority than James Townsend, Esq."

Bodie's harsh winters and Townsend's failing physical condition finally made it impossible for him to continue publishing the newspaper. He sold it to two of his employees in 1899 and moved to Oakland, CA, for the winter. Doten said that he talked about writing an autobiography (which Townsend apparently planned to title *Truth, with Variations*), but with deteriorating eyesight and hearing, and his body wracked with rheumatism and arthritis, Townsend was in no condition to do so. During the summer of 1900, he traveled east to Lake Forest, IL, to stay with his older brother and died there on August 11, 1900. He was sixty-two years old.

6

The Scribe

*To make up respectable local columns was a constant strain on
the mental capacity and legs of the writer, and he had almost
said, "on the imagination," but a strict moral training in early
life, etc. caused him to confine himself strictly to facts.*

~ FRED H. HART ~

UNLIKE MANY OF Nevada's best-known frontier journalists, many of
whom were associated with Virginia City's *Territorial Enterprise,*
Fred H. Hart gained his greatest fame in another nineteenth century–Nevada
mining town, Austin. From 1873 to 1878, Hart served as co-owner and editor
of the town's *Reese River Reveille.* Like many of his contemporaries, Hart
was a prospector himself, who came to the Silver State to make his fortune in mining before turning to journalism. Hart, like Dan De Quille,
had extensive experience in mining. As a result, he was very knowledgeable
about the industry, which made him a reliable writer on the subject.

Little is known about Hart's early life, other than that he was born
in New York in about 1840 (although one obituary placed his birthdate
about eight years earlier) and that he began writing at the age of fourteen,
while working as a printer's apprentice. He traveled west in the early 1860s
to begin prospecting. Hart worked in several White Pine County mining
camps in Nevada before finding more steady pay at frontier newspapers.
Alf Doten, who was a good friend and occasional coworker, said that Hart
wrote letters to the *Reese River Reveille* about those mining camp activities,
using the nom de plume Van Jacquelin.

Before eventually moving to Austin, he contributed to the *Evening
Telegram* in Hamilton, NV, and to the *White Pine News* in Ely, NV. He also
made his way to Carson City, where he served as a special correspondent to

Doten's *Gold Hill Daily News,* covering the Nevada State Legislature (he did so during the 1873, 1875, and 1877 sessions). Similar to Samuel Clemens, who first used his Mark Twain pen name while covering Nevada's territorial legislature, Hart filed his stories in the *News* using the pen name "Toby Green."

In one of the earliest mentions of Green, Doten, clearly with tongue firmly in cheek, wrote, "FAILED TO CONNECT.—The letter from our regular daily Carson correspondent, Toby Green, which should have arrived yesterday, failed to arrive till this morning; therefore we do not publish it. Whose fault was it; Toby or not Toby? That's the question."

Writing as Green, Hart was a witty, wisecracking correspondent who was not afraid to poke fun at pompous politicians and at their often-ponderous political proceedings. For example, in his "LETTER FROM THE CAPITAL" on January 14, 1873, Hart wrote:

> In the Senate to-day, Mr. Phelan [State Senator James Phelan of Storey County] gave notice of a bill providing for the appointment of an inspector of alcoholic liquors. If ever there was need of the creation of an office there is need in this instance. Let a man take two drinks of ordinary Carson whisky and in five minutes afterward he'll fancy that he owns the Capitol, the Warm Springs and the Mint. I think there ought to be a man—with a cast-iron, copper-bottomed stomach—whose duty shall be to examine this rotgut, and throw it "righd avay oud."

About a month later, on February 19, Hart reported that all of Carson City was excited about an upcoming legislative event:

> The entire population of Carson—that is the resident population—are now engaged in anxious preparation for the legislative ball. A splendid time is anticipated, but Toby Green thinks it will be a grand crush. There will be, in all probability, 500 persons present, which is really more than the hall can comfortably accommodate. Mrs. Green was so anxious to attend that I could not refuse my permission and escort; but I have strictly forbidden her to wear that thousand-dollar lace overskirt, as there will be a great many Virginians present, and it might get snatched.

A Social Club Is Born

The Austin that Hart encountered in 1873 was, in his own words, "a small, interior mining town, ninety miles, by a rough road, from the Central Pacific Railroad, having its communication with the outer world carried on by means of mud-wagons, called by courtesy stages; and it can readily be conceived, a quiet place, in which anything of a startling nature in the line of news seldom transpires."

Hart wrote that the town was relatively well run, without much scandal or crime, so the newspaper relied on clippings from other newspapers via the newspaper exchange and on receiving telegraphic news (an early form of newswire services) to supply content. This meant, however, that putting a small daily newspaper together was a near-constant quest for news and feature items to place in the paper.

"To make up respectable local columns was a constant strain on the mental capacity and legs of the writer, and he had almost said, 'on the imagination,' but a strict moral training in early life, etc. caused him to confine himself strictly to facts," Hart explained.

Writing about Hart many years later, Oscar Lewis, who penned an amusing history of Austin titled *The Town That Died Laughing* (which borrowed liberally—and sometimes word for word— from Hart's own writings), said that Hart's editorial duties included "everything in a writing line that needed to be done." These tasks, Lewis explained, ranged from writing and laying out advertisement copy to writing about the important topics of the day, including local news stories, which were sometimes in short supply.

It was on such a slow news day that Hart was sitting in the Sazerac Saloon, a local watering hole named for a popular variety of brandy, hoping to pick up some good gossip or other information that he could use in the local column of the paper. Later writing about his news-gathering challenges, he said:

> I had long had my eye on the place as one liable at any time to pan out the text for a local, and would drop in there nearly every evening and listen to the conversation, in the hope of picking up from it the hoped-for item; but the stories were generally so outrageously devoid of all semblance of truth or appearance of probability, that, as a consistent journalist, whose mission and duty it was to present the public with cold, bald-faced facts, I was unable to reconcile my conscience to the "writing up" and publication of the yarns. On one of these visits I

found the old crowd in the saloon, sitting around the stove as usual, but the orator of the evening was a new man—one well known in the town, although this was his first appearance at the re-unions.

Hart went on to say that the man was noteworthy because his feet were enormous: "They were fearfully and wonderfully made, and their owner had repeatedly refused liberal offers for their use as battery stamps in a quart mill."

The man with the big feet was George Washington Fibley, and he proceeded to tell the assembled audience about having seen a pile of silver bars at a Mexican seaport that was so large, it stretched seven miles long, was forty feet high, and was thirteen feet wide.

"I went out of the saloon, thinking what a magnificent liar this man was, how he had mistaken his vocation, and what a splendid journalist that elastic and towering imagination might make of him," Hart wrote. The following day, he composed a brief item about the man for the *Reveille:* "ELECTED PRESIDENT—The Sazerac Lying Club was organized last night, our esteemed, prominent, and respected fellow-citizen, Mr. George Washington Fibley, being unanimously chosen president of the organization. There was no opposing candidate; his claims and entire fitness for the honorable position being conceded by common consent of the Club."

Hart said that the short article generated considerable amusement among the *Reveille*'s readers—but not for Mr. Fibley, who stormed down to the newspaper offices to demand an apology. Hart said that he agreed to issue a retraction but noted:

> Writing an apology is not a pleasant task for an editor. His soul revolts in it. . .but I had said that would atone in the *Reveille* for the slight cast upon Mr. Fibley's fair fame, and it had to be done. I did it, and the retraction, *verbatim et literatim,* read as follows: "APOLOGETIC—An apology is due from the *Reveille* to Mr. George Washington Fibley. We said in yesterday's issue that he was elected President of the Sazerac Lying Club. This was an error; he was defeated." Mr. Fibley was satisfied, his ruffled feeling modified, and from that time forward we were the best of friends.

With that, Hart explained the creation of his best-known and most long-lived hoax—the Sazerac Lying Club. The club consisted of male members of the Austin community who allegedly met regularly at the Sazerac Saloon to swap fanciful stories. The joke, of course, was that there was no such club and that the tall tales were all invented by Hart.

For the next several years, Hart shared the often-wild tales supposedly told by members of the club. For example, one of the earliest recountings of the club's activities was the story of "Uncle John and the Sage-Hens." Uncle John Gibbons, a veteran stagecoach driver who drove the Austin to Belmont route, "except when laid up with the rheumatism, which periodically attacks him," said that he was delayed one day because of a scourge of sage hens, according to Hart. "He said that while crossing Smoky Valley, a short distance this side of the salt-marsh, he observed what he at first supposed to be a heavy bank of dark clouds descending on the valley. As the stage approached nearer the object, however, he became convinced that the mass was composed of living creatures."

Hart then shifted to telling the tale in Gibbons's own words:

"As I kept gittin' nearer I saw the thing warn't nothin' but a flock of sage-hen; so I jest threw the silk at the leaders, and yelled fire and brimstone to the wheelers, calk'latin to slash the team squar' through the flock without any trouble.

"But, boys, thar was more sage-hen obstructin' of the road than I could reckoned on: and when them thar leaders srruck into them sage-hen, they was throwed back on their ha'nches jest as if they had butted clean up ag'in a stun' wall. . . . Thar I was banked up by a lot of insignificant sage-hen, and the United States mail detained in the big road by feathers."

Gibbons said that his only recourse was to unhitch one of his horses and to ride back to the station for help. Once there, he enlisted the help of several men, including that of a visiting prospector, who grabbed axes in order to return to the wall of birds and to chop a road through the avian mass. The prospector, however, suggested that dynamite might work better, so he packed up his drills, powder cartridges, and fuse, and the group returned to the abandoned stage.

Gibbons then allegedly went on to say, "When we got thar—well I wish I may be runned over by a two-horse jerk-water if thar was a sage-hen in sight as far's as a man could see with a spy-glass," and he finally added, "I hope you fellers is contented now you know what kept the stage late the other night."

Hart frequently gave his narrators descriptive titles rather than names, such as "the Traveler," "the Theological Member," "the Medical Member," "the Fighting Member," "the Doubter," "Mr. Truefact," "the Philosopher," and "Old Reliable." For example, in one column, a reoccurring character called "Old Dad" relates a tale about the strongest man he has ever seen. He says that while mining in Marshall Cañon, he noticed that the windlass-man, who worked the windlass at the top of a 210-foot shaft, was a rather small man who never seemed to weaken. One day, the miners at the bottom of the shaft decided to test him by packing the car with wet clay and then having four men jump on the platform before calling for the smaller man to hoist them up. Hart's narrator reports:

> "She commenced mountin' that shaft just as easy as if a ninety-horse-power engine was hoistin' her out, and every bit of the machinery greased within an inch of its life." "When we got to the surface," said Dad, "we was as ashamed as a dog caught suckin' eggs. Thar was that little fellow, as cool like and as ca'm as one of them icebergs, never sweatin' a ha'r nor puffin' a puff, and a-turnin' the windlass crank with one hand; and as the boys stepped off the car he said, kinder quiet like: 'Boys, can't yer put a load on the car some time? I got dyspepsy, and the doctor told me I must take exercise.'"

Another of Hart's whoppers was designed to poke fun at the enormously wealthy Comstock-mining owners. In this tale, the club's president describes a recent journey to San Francisco when he shared a sleeping car with one of the Comstock bonanza kings:

> The monarch occupied the upper berth and the President the lower. When the latter arrived in San Francisco he felt a peculiar heaviness to his body and limbs, his arms and legs especially being so weighty that he was hardly able to control their motions. He visited a prominent physician, who, after diagnosing his case, told him to go to the Hammam, a bathing establishment of that name, and get "retorted." He accordingly went to that establishment and took a Turkish bath; and when his pores began to open, silver oozed out of his body, like

quicksilver going through a rag. Although, he cleaned up a bar valued
at $417.92 and a fraction. He says the silver must have oozed into him
from the bonanza king in the berth above, that night on the sleeper.

Not all who applied for membership in the Sazerac Lying Club were
accepted, according to Hart's humorous reports. On one occasion, he
claimed, the organization had received an application from a newspaper
editor from San Francisco:

"Hold!" exclaimed Old Dad; "them newspaper fellers can't lie." "I beg
to differ with the gentleman," remarked the Doubter. "I was readin' of
an account in a paper this mornin' relatin' of a occurrence whereby a
young lady run a needle into her foot a great many years ago and after
she had got married and her children had got married and had children, that thar needle one day came out of the top of one of her grand-
children's head—a leetle bit rusted, of course, but the same identical
needle. Now if that aint a lie, I'd like to know what you call it."

The club decided not to admit editors on the grounds that the
membership should be kept upon an amateur basis.

As Hart was nearing the end of his time in Austin, he was approached
by a San Francisco publisher, Henry Keller, who wanted him to compile his
Lying Club entries into a book. Not surprisingly, while happily accepting
the offer, Hart incorporated the book proposal into his tales—perhaps one
of the earliest examples of an author going meta:

The Chair handed the Secretary an envelope, from which that official
extracted a sheet of letter paper, and read it as follows:

Austin, Nevada, November 20th, 1877

TO THE PRESIDENT AND MEMBERS OF THE SAZERAC LYING CLUB
Gentlemen: As you may be personally and officially aware, I have, in
my capacity of editor of the *Daily Reese River Reveille,* been divers and
sundry times called upon to record in my valuable, wide circulated, and
strictly family journal, some of the proceedings of the Club of which
you have the distinguished honor to be President and members. This
circumstance has caused the fame of the Sazerac Lying Club to spread
abroad over this land of liberty, and even across the great waters to the

ends thereof. Yes, Mr. President and gentlemen, your fame and renown have spread like the exhalations of the upas tree, or a Chinese umbrella, or a Chicago girl's feet, or a church scandal, or anything else that has a habit of spreading; until at last it has even reached unto San Francisco.

I am in receipt of a communication from a firm of San Francisco publishers, requesting me to endeavor to obtain access to the archives and records of your Club, and to extract therefrom such matter as I, in judgement, may select, the same to be published by the said firm in the form of a book, that the Sazerac Lying Club may be perpetuated unto our children, and our children's children, and to other generations yet unborn. My object therefore, in thus addressing your most honorable body, is to obtain the permission as herein set forth for the purpose above stated, and to enable me to comply with the request embodied in the proceeding.

Hart went on to say that after the official had read the request, the club deliberated for some time before deciding to allow the *Reveille's* editor access to all of the club's records and archives for the book. In the culmination of his clever piece, he added that John Gibbons followed up with a resolution stating that "reporters should not be admitted at future sessions of the Club, and that all future records of proceedings be chucked into the stove as soon as recorded. This was unanimously adopted, as was a resolution by Old Dad, that the sessions of the Sazerac Lying Club be conducted with closed doors, NOW AND FOREVER AFTER."

And with that, Hart concluded the proceedings of the Sazerac Lying Club.

Published in 1878, *The Sazerac Lying Club: A Nevada Book,* was popular enough to go through at least five printings. It contained not only Hart's Lying Club entries—complete with engraved images of the fictional participants—but also other examples of his writing, including frontier sketches about Nevada, a chapter about living in a mining town, and other observations. Even the dedication reflected Hart's unique sense of humor: "To each and every person who may purchase it, and pay cash for it, this volume is respectfully dedicated, by THE AUTHOR."

Literary historian Ella Sterling Cummins described the book as follows: "Humor, grotesque and characteristic, play over the pages. Local color is laid on unsparingly, well known individuals are cartooned and immortalized. The atmosphere of Nevada, the glory of the sunsets, pictures of the mining town and its people, customs and manners, all are here so vividly portrayed that it is almost panoramic. To one who has ever lived in these climes the volume is a source of unfailing amusement."

Like James Townsend, Hart was occasionally the subject of humorous items appearing in other newspapers. For instance, in February 1877 the *Pioche Record* printed a fake biography that included these details:

> Mr. Hart informs us that he was born in Ireland in 1810, of poor but honest parents, and is now 67 years of age. He immigrated to the United States forty years ago, and commenced business as devil in a large printing establishment. He came to this coast in '49, and has lived in every town, city and hamlet both in Nevada and California. Fred doesn't look as old as he is, in consequences of having lost all his flesh in the mines of Eastern Nevada, but is now a very animated skeleton. Mr. Hart was for a long time editor of the Austin *Reveille,* and made a lasting name as a humorist, his bon-mots being copied in all of the papers of this coast and in many of the Eastern papers. Fred has a laughing black eye and a decidedly Roman nose. He is about 4 feet 3 in height, and has no circumference whatever. He is a genial cuss and as smart as a steel trap. As "Toby Green" he has appeared in the *Gold Hill Daily News* during every session of the Legislature, and is really a small specimen of concentrated wit and fun.

Moving On

In 1878 Hart sold his ownership stake in the *Reveille* to his partner, James Booth, in order to complete his book. Following its publication, he continued working as a special correspondent in Carson City for Alf Doten at the *Gold Hill Daily News,* and then he spent some time in Eureka, NV, ("Not doing too much," according to Doten) before being offered the editorship of the *Territorial Enterprise* in 1880. His tenure was, in Doten's words, "remarkably brilliant as well as brief." Writing in *The Nevada Magazine* in 1899, Doten described what happened:

> Inspiration of some kind got into him one evening to distinguish himself editorially, and he did most effectively succeed. James G. Fair was running for United State Senator from Nevada, so Fred devoted to him one long, two-column, pungent, paragraphic editorial, headed, "Slippery Jim," ridiculing his ability or capability as a would-be states-

man, and relating sundry current anecdotes of his alleged surreptitious mining methods and sly trickeries among his miners and mankind generally, both above and below ground.

The editorial caught the eye of John Mackay, half owner of the *Territorial Enterprise* and longtime business partner of James Fair, and he threatened to fire Hart. Apparently, Mackay was persuaded by influential friends not to follow through on his threat, so Hart remained as editor but with little room for error in the future. Doten said that about a month later, "an east wind from the brewery struck him again," and Hart crafted "a long-winded, viciously crotchety editorial, like that on Fair," exposing the misdeeds of the Alta Mining Company, a prominent Virginia City mining firm and one of the *Enterprise*'s largest advertisers and patrons. Doten reported:

> There was a cloudburst, earthquake and war-dance, all in one, next morning when the Alta folks and their friends, waving aloft their gleaming machetes and tomahawks, came charging down upon the *"Enterprise"* office with blood in their eyes. Poor little Fred Hart got wind of the coming cyclone, and struck out through the sagebrush across the north end of the Mount Davidson range with great alacrity, never stopping till safe on San Francisco's beautiful shore. His journalistic ship was wrecked forever, and he drifted about, picking up little jobs of reporting by way of precarious subsistence.

By all accounts, Hart did, indeed, wander off to San Francisco, where he is believed to have played a part in the founding of the *San Francisco Daily Stock Report* newspaper in 1880. By 1884 his byline was appearing in San Francisco's *Daily Exchange* newspaper, and then, starting in May 1887, he relocated to California's capital city to become editor of *The Sacramento Star* newspaper. In this latter post, he was, according to the *Elko Independent,* "putting in considerable attic salt in its columns." He only held that job for a short time, with the *Star* announcing on July 25, 1887: "It is with regret that we are called upon to state that Fred Hart, who has been the editor for several months, has resigned his position on the Star in order to accept a more lucrative position." The paper did not, however, indicate what that more lucrative position might be, and there is no indication that Hart was anything more than an occasional correspondent for various newspapers in Northern California during the next decade.

One of the last reports about Hart appeared in Alf Doten's June 24, 1896, diary entry: "Met Fred Hart on the street [in Carson City]—arrived from San F[rancisco] this morning—Had long old-time chat with him—looks aged, seedy, and unhealthy."

An obituary in *The San Francisco Call* on September 1, 1897, said that Hart had died the day before of Bright's disease (a kidney ailment) in the county hospital in Sacramento. The item claimed that he had "resided in Sacramento for several years, and wrote for the local papers" prior to his death. It noted that he was the author of *The Sazerac Lying Club,* which had gained him some fame, that he had been a friend and contemporary of Mark Twain, and that he had been "at one time one of the best-known newspaper men on the Pacific Coast." At the time of his death, Hart was fifty-seven years old and left behind a wife and two boys, ages thirteen and fifteen. His body was interred at the Cypress Lawn Cemetery in San Francisco.

Like many pioneer editors and reporters, Hart struggled with alcoholism. The *Sacramento Union's* account of his death noted:

Fred H. Hart died yesterday at the County Hospital, where he had been ill for some time. He was familiarly known as "Fred Hart" in all the business section, where for years he had been seen upon the streets, and excited no little commiseration because of the unhappy habit that wrecked what was once a most promising life. It is said that he was a sufferer to an extent that drove him to drink. At least it is the charitable cover of pity, for Hart had often declared that he was his own worst enemy.

Fred Hart had other faults than indulgence of appetite: who has not? But these were of minor character; let the grave cover them all now. A bright, capable, useful man has gone the way of many. The slender, unkempt figure of the little old man will be seen no more upon the streets, where it had long attracted attention. For Hart had that about him, despite his evident enslavement, which commanded attention. It was intelligence, brains not wholly quenched; capacity still asserting itself.

In August 1835 *The New York Sun* newspaper published a series of stories claiming that the moon was inhabited by bat-like moon people, such as the ones depicted here, and by other amazing creatures. Public domain/originally appeared in *The New York Sun*, August 25, 1835.

On January 29, 1934, the *Los Angeles Times* published an article about so-called "Lizard People" living in catacombs beneath the city. Public domain.

According to the January 29, 1934, edition of the *Los Angeles Times*, mining engineer G. Warren Shufelt (pictured here) had invented a "radio X-ray" device that detected a vast underground system of tunnels beneath Los Angeles inhabited by "Lizard People." Courtesy of *Los Angeles Times* Photographic Archive, Library Special Collections, Charles E. Young Research Library, UCLA.

Several of the Comstock region's most renowned editors and reporters posed for this photo in 1869, including (*left to right*): William Gillespie of the *Territorial Enterprise*; Charles Parker of the *Gold Hill Evening News*; Dan De Quille of the *Enterprise*; Robert Lowery of the *Virginia Daily Union*; and Alfred Doten of the *Enterprise*. Courtesy of Special Collections and University Archives Department, University of Nevada, Reno.

View of the composing room at the *Territorial Enterprise*, taken in 1947. Courtesy of Special Collections and University Archives Department, University of Nevada, Reno.

Mark Twain, undated. Courtesy of US National Archives.

Mark Twain, between 1860 and 1870. Courtesy of Special Collections and University Archives Department, University of Nevada, Reno.

Portrait of William Wright (Dan De Quille), taken between 1860 and 1880. Courtesy of Special Collections and University Archives Department, University of Nevada, Reno.

Image of "Lying Jim" Townsend that appeared in the *Overland Monthly* in 1915. Public domain/appeared in *Overland Monthly*, August 1915.

Depiction of the Sazerac Lying Club in session, which appeared in Fred Hart's *The Sazerac Lying Club* book, published in 1878. Book and photo in public domain.

Overview of Austin, NV, in 1867, taken from a hill overlooking the thriving mining camp. Courtesy of Special Collections and University Archives Department, University of Nevada, Reno.

Samuel Post Davis, longtime editor of the *Carson Daily Appeal*. Courtesy of Special Collections and University Archives Department, University of Nevada, Reno.

Alfred "Alf" Doten, who maintained diaries of his daily activities for more than half a century. Courtesy of Special Collections and University Archives Department, University of Nevada, Reno.

Newspaper editor William J. Forbes, also known as "Semblins." Courtesy of Special Collections and University Archives Department, University of Nevada, Reno.

Masthead of the *Tuscarora Times-Review* when Major John Dennis served as editor.

Portrait of Joseph Goodman.
Courtesy of Special
Collections and University
Archives Department,
University of Nevada, Reno.

Eureka Sentinel Building, circa 1940s. Courtesy of the Library of Congress.

The *Territorial Enterprise* building in 1937. Courtesy of the Library of Congress.

Photo believed to be of Julia Bulette. Courtesy of the Nevada Historical Society.

Portrait of Lucius Beebe, who owned the *Territorial Enterprise* in the 1950s. Courtesy of Special Collections and University Archives Department, University of Nevada, Reno.

Lucius Beebe (*seated*) and Charles Clegg in their office, examining a copy of the *Territorial Enterprise*. Courtesy of the California State Railroad Museum.

7

The Polymath

My imagination is not sluggish, and so I manufacture all I write.

~ SAMUEL POST DAVIS ~

S AM DAVIS WAS not content to be merely a journalist or just an editor. Or just a newspaper owner. Or just a rancher. Or just a poet, a playwright, an actor, a politician, a lecturer, an essayist, a short-story writer, or a historian. In fact, during his sixty-eight years, Davis managed to pack in all of those professions—and more.

Although he was nearly two decades younger than Sam Clemens and Dan De Quille, Davis carried on many of the same types of journalistic pranks that they were known for, including fake feuds with rival newspaper editors (even going so far as to concoct a fake rival newspaper) and cleverly crafted hoaxes.

THE STORY OF THE *WABUSKA MANGLER*

Perhaps Davis's best-known punk was his creation of the *Wabuska Mangler*, a newspaper that he alleged was published by Edward P. Lovejoy in the small community of Wabuska, near Yerington, NV. Starting in 1889, Davis started printing small, often sarcastic rants about Lovejoy and the *Mangler* in the *Carson Daily Appeal*. The real Lovejoy, a former California newspaper owner and editor, prominent Wabuska businessman, frequent *Appeal* advertiser, and friend of Davis's, apparently did not object to the mostly gentle ribbing, which began in April 1889, when Davis noted in a news brief that "Editor Lovejoy, of the *Wabuska Mangler*, has added another column to his live paper."

Lovejoy was the son of Elijah Parrish Lovejoy, an Illinois minister, abolitionist, and newspaper owner who was murdered in 1837 while protecting his printing press from a proslavery mob. (The younger Lovejoy's connection to the famed abolitionist remained relatively unknown until it was discovered by William G. Chrystal, who wrote about the association in the spring 1994 issue of the *Nevada Historical Quarterly.*) The son relocated to California, where he became a lawyer, the district attorney for Trinity County in California, a county judge, and a newspaper publisher and editor. In 1877 he moved to Virginia City, where he began working for the Carson & Colorado Railway, and he eventually became its agent in Wabuska. He did well there, opening a general store and a bar that primarily served railroad passengers. Eventually he became the town's postmaster and owned a 1,500-acre ranch with horses and cattle.

A few days after Davis had published his first *Mangler* entry, he followed up with a longer piece that poked fun at Lovejoy:

> THE WABUSKA MANGLER—About six months ago a man came to this office from Wabuska and purchased a lot of old damaged pica type on tick, and a Washington hand press with half the parts gone. He then started the *Mangler* and with the old type, not yet paid for, began denouncing the *Appeal* editor as a political refugee from Iceland and an enemy of the commonwealth. We hope the old lair who runs the *Mangler* will come up here and settle for his type and return the melting pot he borrowed of us to make roller composition in. Last week we caught him stealing an electro-type of George Washington and he agreed to return it as soon as he ran his weekly off, so that we can have it in time for the centennial issue. He still holds on to it as he never lets go of anything that he once gets his claws on. The *Mangler,* however, is six months old today and one of the spiciest of our country exchanges.

A day later, Davis reached back into his bag of *Mangler* tricks and wrote: "E. P. Lovejoy, publisher of the *Wabuska Mangler,* came to town last night to get a few pounds of glue and molasses composition for his old press. We hate to trust these country editors any way, but when he asked us for the goods he drew a 14-inch bowie-knife out of his boot. We smiled and said he was good for anything we had in the shop. Lovejoy is a live journalist and a man we always like to meet."

In September 1889 Davis wrote yet another humorous entry in the long-running gag: "Hank Snaggs, the man charged with throwing pole cats [skunks] into the sanctum of the *Wabuska Mangler,* writes that the editor treated him to a cocktail next morning on the ground that the pole cats carried him back on memory's wing to his boyhood days in Missouri. No hard feeling now exists between Snaggs and the *Mangler*'s scribe."

Davis even incorporated his friend into testimonial advertisements, such as this one: "Mr. E. P. Lovejoy, a large dealer in general merchandise, and editor of the *Wabuska Mangler*, at Wabuska, NV, says: 'I have tried St. Patrick's Pills and can truthfully say they are the best I have ever taken or known need.' As a pleasant physic or for disorders of the liver they will always give perfect satisfaction. For sale by G. C. Thaxter."

One of Davis's more elaborate tales about the *Mangler* appeared in May 1890, when he wrote:

> HARD EDITORIAL LINES—The *Wabuska Mangler* of Friday says: Last week as the *Mangler* was going to press, Sol Noel's Holstein bull came charging into the office and demolished the forms so that we were unable to get the issue out until today. We are well aware of the fact that the *Mangler* in this section is a great annoyance to the good many men here who would like to run politics to suit themselves. We know for a fact that for some months past, Sol Noel and a lot of his conferees have been training the bull to charge into print shops. They rigged up an old cider press and fixed a lever on it so as to represent the *Mangler* press and a man would stand on the side and make motions as if running an ink roller over the forms. They would then flaunt a red flag in the bull's face and let him charge on the machine and knock it over. He would then be fed real hay as his reward for his success in demolishing an educational machine. They got the bull well in train and then sent it charging into our office with the above result. He went home with his hide filled with No. 8 shot and if any of the gang come here again they will be treated to something a little heavier. We will continue to publish the *Mangler* and show up political iniquity whenever it can be found. We will begin suit against Noel in the Justice Court tomorrow for back subscription and damages.

In April 1891 Davis explained that the *Mangler* was starting up again after being snowbound during the winter months:

> Mr. Lovejoy the publisher was in the city making arrangements to resuscitate the journal. He has added to his stock by purchasing some of the old *Dayton Times* material and is now negotiating with the

Appeal for the casting of a roller. As soon as it is finished and reaches Wabuska by slow freight the sheet will resume the libeling of Lovejoy's neighbors and in general blackguarding of the residents of Mason Valley. As a newspaper the *Mangler* is a regular Joe Dandy, built some-what on the lines laid down by the *Homer Index.*

The editor has been slinging mud at the *Appeal* for some years, but whenever he wants any first-class rollers made, so that his old sheet can be distinguished from a three weeks old piece of fly paper, he runs his face for the material at this office and never pays a bean. The sheet will be run as a Farmers Alliance organ this summer and in the winter go whatever way the swag seems the easiest to reach. We welcome it to our exchange list, and have invited the publisher to consider himself at home in our office whenever he is not in the Police Station.

In August 1891 the teasing ended when Lovejoy unexpectedly passed away. Davis wrote a properly respectful notice about the death of his friend:

News was received in Carson yesterday of the sudden death of E. P. Lovejoy of Wabuska, Lyon County. His death was the result of heart disease and so unexpected that his wife was in Virginia at the time. He was one of the most enterprising men in the State and always was endeavoring to develop its resources. He will be greatly missed in Mason Valley. He kept a grocery and hotel there and in early life was a newspaper publisher.

Interestingly, Davis shared a number of traits with Lovejoy. Born in 1850 in Bradford, CT, he, too, was the son of a religious man: his father was an Episcopal priest. Davis, himself, had actually studied theology at Racine College before dropping out to become a journalist (he also had two younger brothers, Robert and William, who had long and successful careers in journalism). He pursued his own writing career in several places, includ-ing Nebraska, Missouri, and Chicago, before heading to California, where he worked at the *Vallejo Independent,* the *San Francisco Chronicle,* the *Daily Evening Post, The Morning Ledger* (the last two also in San Francisco), and other publications.

While working in Vallejo, Davis concocted one of his most long-lived hoaxes. In the early 1870s he was publishing a small publication called *Open Letter.* One night over dinner, he boasted to a friend, Woodford Owens, that he could imitate any modern writer easily. Owens responded by wagering a wine and oyster dinner that Davis could not imitate the writing of Bret Harte, the popular poet and journalist. Fired up to win the bet, Davis quickly wrote a short poem, "Binley and '46,'" in Harte's writing style, which he published in the *Open Letter*. He included a brief note saying that the poem had been discovered in an old trunk that Harte had left in a San Francisco lodging house. The *Open Letter* claimed that the poem was signed by Harte and was written in his handwriting.

The poem describes an engineer who attempts to push his train through a terrible snowstorm in the Sierra Nevada but who ends up dying at his post, with his frozen hand still on the throttle. Newspapers all over the country published the dramatic poem, which even appeared in *Frank Leslie's Illustrated Newspaper* in New York in May 1874, with Harte's byline, as well as in several books collecting Harte's works. It should be noted that Owens honored the wager.

The September 1902 issue of the *Overland Monthly*, a San Francisco-based magazine, reported that Davis had eventually revealed the truth in a subsequent issue of the *Open Letter:* "For the next sixty days there was a turmoil throughout newspaperdom. Mr. Davis was complimented by some of the critics on being a better poet than Harte and savagely assailed by others for his audacity in daring to use the name of so distinguished a writer, in order to get his work before the public. . . . Despite all the discussion which was waged on the subject Harte was simply an amused looker on, and has never been recorded as having given utterance to the slightest expression on the subject."

A close reading of the poem does provide a clue that the author did not intend for it to be taken too seriously. While the overall tone of the poem is very dramatic, the narrator establishes early on that Binley, the engineer, has plenty of fuel and that "his furnace burns with a fiercer glow"; yet once Binley encounters the unyielding snow drifts that stop his locomotive in its tracks, he simply gives up and freezes to death.

AN APPEALING OPPORTUNITY

In 1875, A few years before his tenure at the *Carson Daily Appeal* began, Davis moved to Virginia City and worked as a reporter for the *Virginia City Evening Chronicle,* which was owned and edited at the time by Denis McCarthy (a previous co-owner of the *Territorial Enterprise,* along with Joseph Goodman and Jonathan Williams). In 1879 Davis became editor of the *Appeal,* a position he would hold for the next two decades. The *Appeal* had just lost its well-respected owner and editor, Henry Rust Mighels, who had also served in the Nevada State Assembly and who had recently died. After Mighels's death, his widow, Nellie Verrill Mighels—a talented reporter in her own right, the first woman to cover the Nevada Legislature, and the only female reporter to cover the Corbett-Fitzsimmons fight in Carson City in 1897—hired Davis to oversee the paper.

Within a short time, Davis began to enhance the *Appeal*'s reputation by embarking on investigations into public corruption and by promoting the public good. He was outspoken on a number of topics, for example, harshly criticizing insurance companies for not fulfilling their promise to pay for damages caused by the great San Francisco earthquake in 1906. Historian Lawrence Berkove noted that Davis, "acting unilaterally as ex officio state insurance commissioner, announced that any insurance companies that did not pay 100 cents on the dollar in California would not be allowed to do business in Nevada." The ploy worked, after several other states followed suit, and solvent insurance companies agreed to pay up.

On July 4, 1880, Davis married Nellie Mighels and became co-owner of the *Appeal,* continuing to also serve as editor (while helping to raise four stepchildren, as well as the two daughters—Lucy Davis Crowell and Ethel Davis Waite—whom he had with Nellie). That same year he also found time to publish a mock obituary for one of his good friends, Rollin M. Daggett, who had just become an editor at the *Territorial Enterprise* (the *Enterprise* was owned at the time by Senator William Sharon; Sharon's periodic business partner, Darius Ogden Mills, who co-owned the Virginia and Truckee Railroad with the senator, is also mentioned in the fake obit):

> Rollin M. Daggett was found lying stiff and stark near the Base Range, killed by Cassidy and Jim Fair, who hacked him to pieces early in the fight and left the mutilated remains upon the field. Sharon and D. O Mills sent these men to their work and it was the coin of the C. P. Railroad that helped to bear the brave soldier to earth.
>
> Looking upon his remains we recall the observation which the King made over the body of Falstaff: "I might have better spared a better man."

In 1880 Davis also crafted another hoax, which appeared in the *Appeal* and was reprinted in dozens of newspapers throughout the country, initially titled "Mark Twain and Dan De Quille" but later titled "The Typographical Howitzer." The farcical tale recounted Twain and De Quille's much-earlier decision to start a newspaper in Mendocino, CA. In Davis's story, the two men packed up type and other equipment from a recently defunct newspaper that they had run in San Francisco, loaded it all in a wagon, and headed into the wilds of Northern California. The two also took along a small mountain howitzer, which Twain planned to fire off to celebrate the start of their paper.

While camping on the first night of their journey, they encountered a group of Native Americans and feared the worst. Twain suggested loading the cannon with powder and firing it to scare off the anticipated attackers. When a group of about fifty Native Americans rushed the camp, De Quille shoved something into the mouth of the gun and then yelled for Twain to fire it.

At this point there was a loud explosion, followed by cries of pain. Twain asked De Quille what he had jammed into the cannon, and the latter responded, "A column of solid nonpareil and a couple of sticks of your spring poetry." Twain then suggested that they reload and use one of De Quille's "geological articles." When the intruders rushed again, De Quille began loading the howitzer with the lead type from a variety of poems, articles, and advertisements.

"That poetry, reaching 'em first, will throw 'em into confusion, and my editorial, coming upon the heels of the rest, will result in a lasting demoralization. It will be like the last cavalry charge of the French at the battle of Austerlitz," De Quille was quoted as saying.

After Twain fired the howitzer three times, the survivors of the attack fled. He and De Quille then surveyed the bloody scene, described in gruesome detail in Davis's account. "The pen is mightier than the sword," proclaimed one of the journalists. The other responded, "You bet. Hurrah for Faust and Gutenberg." Having used up all of their type, however, the two were left with nothing to start a paper. According to Davis, they "reached Virginia City, weary, discouraged, and foot sore, and secured a place on the *Enterprise*."

In addition to writing such absurdist pieces and editing the *Appeal*, Davis found time to craft articles for other publications, such as the *Argonaut*, a literary newspaper in San Francisco. And in 1894 he contributed another fake tale, "Serious Trifling," to the *San Francisco Midwinter Appeal*. In this story, Davis recounted how in the early days of Virginia City, it was customary for people to gather together to offer testimonials to public men. He said that several years earlier, the superintendent of one of the better-known mines had been successful, so his friends decided to chip in money to purchase him a gold watch and chain, which they planned to present to him at a testimonial event. Wanting to keep it a surprise, they did not tell him but instead sent him a tongue-in-cheek note, ordering him to appear at the mining company offices at 7:30 PM "to answer to certain grave charges which have been made against your official conduct in connection with the superintendency of the mine."

Davis said that about a hundred of the man's friends gathered at the assigned time for the presentation, which featured baskets of wine set out for the party. "At half-past seven, however there was no superintendent," he continued. "Eight o'clock came, and he was not there. Half an hour later some friends went to his room to see if he had received the note. He had received it and JUMPED THE TOWN."

Another Davis fake-news item appeared in the *San Francisco Morning Call* in October 1895. Titled "When Booth Was Not Booth," it's a first-person account of an episode that most likely was greatly embellished but which is told with such certainty as to make it believable. The story, which incorporates the names of real individuals in the San Francisco theater scene, tells of a down-and-out actor who, through the machinations of Davis and a friend, imitates the legendary actor Edwin Booth (who was the brother of the notorious John Wilkes Booth, the man who assassinated President Lincoln in 1865) during a performance of *Hamlet.* The actor is said to sound like and to greatly resemble Booth, and his performance is so convincing that the audience and critics are taken in by the ruse. The real Booth, however, shows up near the end of the performance and replaces the actor for the final scenes. In the end, Booth is amused by the deception, the audience and critics have been enthralled, but the actor is miserable, apparently because he did not receive the recognition that he had sought.

In 1886 Davis published his only book, a collection titled *Short Stories.* Sylvia Crowell Stoddard, who was Davis's granddaughter, described him as "so lazy about gathering together his things for publication that it took his friend Ambrose Bierce months of constant nagging before he could make Sam compile the stories, newspaper yarns, and poems which finally comprised this little volume."

Among the tales included in the book is "A Christmas Carol" (often called "The First Piano in Camp"), which is perhaps his most-reprinted and most-enduring work. The story, which originally appeared in the *Virginia City Evening Chronicle* in the early 1870s, is a finely crafted account of a "pianner" arriving in the mining town of Pioche, NV, but no one knows how to play it. A stranger suddenly appears on Christmas Eve and gives the community a memorable concert.

Davis was far more committed when it came to his politics. While at the *Appeal,* he became a student of state and federal monetary policy and was influential in the formation of the Silver Party, which promoted remonetizing silver and moving away from solely backing US currency with gold. His editorials also reflected his playful take on the politics of the time, for example, this tongue-in-cheek message in 1894: "It is thought nothing amiss to resurrect the dead and vote them by wholesale. So long as the memory of the departed is respected by voting him in proper alignment with the party with which he affiliated in his lifetime, the ethics are considered as not having been violated. Hon. William Sharon was accorded the credit of having invaded the cemetery for primary votes, but he has no patent on this method."

In 1898 Davis stepped down from his job as editor of the *Appeal* in order to run for Nevada state controller on the Silver Party ticket. He would go on to serve for eight years in this office (winning reelection in 1902), and he then served for another four years as the state publicity commissioner, a job that today might be akin to heading up the state tourism department.

Writing About "Sumpthin" Peculiar

His foray into the political arena did not, however, squelch Davis's creative impulses or his mischievous streak. In 1901 he published one of his most famous fake stories, "The Mystery of the Savage Sump," in the pages of *The Black Cat* magazine. Literary scholar Berkove described the tale, which was reprinted as a booklet and which also appeared in newspapers around the world, including in New Zealand, as "a peculiar combination of fictitious literary hoax about a financial hoax and a realistic exposé." Davis created a new fake story by embellishing an earlier one by De Quille, but the tale was a thinly disguised attack on the Silver King, US senator James G. Fair, one of the Comstock's richest but most avaricious and unscrupulous mine owners.

The story began by stating that the mystery had begun more than two decades earlier, when miners had discovered a bloated body floating in the hot waters of a sump deep in the bowels of the Savage Mine in Virginia City. It noted that hot, scalding water flowed through the depths of Virginia

City's mines and needed to be pumped into such sumps, or catch basins. The story's narrator said that the body had been unrecognizable but that the corpse had still been garbed in a fine pair of boots and clothing, which indicated that the deceased had not been a miner but had still been someone of means. Despite the best efforts of authorities, the body had never been identified, and the mystery had remained unsolved—until now.

"As the years passed the incident was well-nigh forgotten, but now, at this remote time, I am able to furnish the world with a complete solution," Davis wrote. He continued his yarn by noting that the late 1860s and early 1870s was a time of great fluctuations in the mining stock market in San Francisco. He said that in the fall of 1869, William Meeker, a San Francisco stock speculator who had lost a lot of money, was spending a few weeks at Lake Tahoe and decided to go fishing in a small boat. He noticed a swirling funnel of water in the lake, which indicated that water was draining through an opening at the bottom of the lake.

Meeker shared his discovery with another man, Colonial Clair (which, not coincidentally, rhymes with Fair), who was known to be "one of the heaviest and most unscrupulous operators in the market." The two cooked up a plan to see if the draining water was the same water that was flooding the deepest parts of Virginia City's mines. After determining that this was the case, the two began manipulating the flow of the water into the Savage Mine by using a sophisticated plugging system. This permitted Clair to successfully game the mining stock market because the value of Savage Mine stock would rise when the water disappeared and the mine became more accessible, and the value would fall when water reappeared. Despite making a fortune with the scheme, Clair's greed got the better of him, and so he murdered Meeker and disposed of his body in the hole at the bottom of Lake Tahoe, where it was sucked into the sump in the Savage Mine.

Making History

Starting in about 1910, Davis next turned his attention to one of the most ambitious projects that he would undertake in his lifetime, editing the massive, two-volume, 1,279-page *History of Nevada*. Published in 1913, the work was a comprehensive, updated look at the state's past, which had previously been told in Thompson & West's *History of Nevada* (1881) and in Thomas Wren's *A History of the State of Nevada: Its Resources and People* (1904). Davis worked with more than two dozen writers, each familiar with their respective subjects, to cover a broad array of topics, including the history of mining, Nevada's political history, and key fraternal organizations.

While visiting in San Francisco in 1917, Davis suffered a stroke, which necessitated the amputation of one of his legs. Davis's granddaughter Stoddard said, "He must have known he was dying, however, because he begged to return to his beloved Nevada to live his last days on the Larkswood Ranch he loved so much." Davis died at his ranch in Carson City on March 17, 1918, and is buried in Lone Mountain Cemetery in Carson City.

8

The Diarist

*Considering age, and sparcity of population as compared with extent
of territory, Nevada, since her admission to the American Union as the
"Battle Born State," in 1864, has produced or utilized more newspapers and
journalists, good, bad or indifferent, than any other of her sister States.*

~ ALFRED DOTEN ~

FOR MORE THAN fifty years Alfred "Alf" Doten kept track of his daily life. He recorded just about *everything*. He wrote about his financial situation, his work at various Comstock-area newspapers, his friends, his meals, his propensity to regularly overindulge in alcohol, and his theater-viewing habits. His diaries—seventy-nine in all—offer some of the best snapshots ever created of life in the nineteenth-century West.

Doten was born on July 21, 1829, in Plymouth, Massachusetts, and his parents were direct descendants of the Mayflower Pilgrims. The eighth of nine children, Doten attended school in Plymouth and then, at the age of 19, signed on to a converted whaling ship, the *Yeoman*, for a 198-day voyage to San Francisco. He made his first entry in his daily diary on March 18, 1849, while voyaging around South America's Cape Horn, and he continued writing in it almost every day until his death in 1903.

Once in California, Doten headed to the Gold Country to see if he could strike it rich. After spending several years largely prospecting in Northern California, he traveled to the Nevada Territory near the end of 1862 to take advantage of promising new discoveries there. His career in newspapers began shortly after his arrival, when he began contributing reports from the mining camp of Como (located in the hills above Dayton) to the *Como Sentinel* and the *Virginia City Daily Union* and sending regular letters to his hometown newspaper, *The Plymouth Rock and Old Colony Reporter*.

By 1864 he had become editor of the *Daily Union,* covering news at the same time as Mark Twain and Dan De Quille. In his diary he noted that on March 6, 1864, he met "Mark Twain—had pleasant chat with him—went up to [J D] Winters room and had a drink together—came down and all took dinner together. . .was in Cross's to supper—had another long chat with M Twain."

THE APRIL FOOLS' DAY "SELL"

Two years later Doten joined the staff of the *Territorial Enterprise,* and while he was generally a serious and conservative writer, he did participate in some playful hoaxes, contributing what was perhaps his best-known fake-news story to the paper on April 1, 1866 (April Fools' Day, appropriately). The short item claimed that a large, reddish-colored bear and three cubs had been captured near the Carson Sink and had been placed inside a building behind Piper's Saloon, where the animals awaited safe transport to San Francisco. In his diary he claimed that his "sell" had fooled some five hundred people, who had stopped by Piper's the next day to see the bears.

Doten was proud enough of his hoax that he also shared the story, albeit with an admission that he had pulled a fast one, in his report to *The Plymouth Rock and Old Colony Reporter* on April 19:

> First thing in the morning, in the local columns of the *Enterprise,* there appeared a very innocent looking, but somewhat startling item, to the effect that a large female cinnamon bear, with three cubs, had just been captured near the sink of Carson River, some twenty-five miles from here, by a couple of soldiers belonging to Fort Churchill, and brought to this city about 9 o'clock the previous evening, en route for San Francisco, and placed temporarily for safe keeping in a small building at the rear of Piper's saloon, which is a prominent place of resort in the heart of the city. The details of the capture were given, and the item wound up with giving the weight of the bears. The old she one weighed 1,300 pounds, and the cubs, which were but two months old, weighed 1,100 pounds each. Now the item looked reasonable enough, except that cinnamon bears always live in the mountains, and never fool away their time out in the deserts and plains. And then too, no one ever saw a bear of that species weighing half so much, to say nothing of those "hefty" little cubs; yet no one person in a dozen stopped to consider such points, but rushed up bald-headed to see "those bears."

It is estimated that nearly a thousand persons, including several ladies, go thus humbugged. Passing through the saloon and opening the rear door, the *bear*-faced sell was made apparent, and shouts of laughter assailed the victims as they came out. Of course the saloon keeper did a very good business, for most of those who got sold took it in good part, and "stood the drinks" manfully. Some men came several miles to "see the bears."

THE PRANKSTERS

Some literary scholars believe that Doten's greatest hoax, however, was in telling the "true" origin of Samuel Clemens's pen name to anyone who expressed curiosity about the famous author's time in Virginia City. As Twain scholar James E. Caron noted, "*Enterprise* colleague Alf Doten would pretend to new acquaintances that 'Mark Twain' meant ordering two drinks on credit, which Clemens supposedly did frequently." While there is plenty of scholarship supporting the notion that the nom de plume actually had its roots in Twain's tendency to buy drinks on credit, the issue remains unresolved—so perhaps Doten did have the last laugh.

Twain's official biographer, Albert Bigelow Paine, recounted another anecdote involving the two writers, which he credited to one of Alf Doten's sons. According to Paine in *Mark Twain, A Biography*, Alf Doten, who was working at the *Gold Hill Daily News*, and Twain, who was working for the *Enterprise*, were assigned by their respective newspapers to head to the mining camp of Como to report on new mining activity in the district. In this story, the two apparently had not met before but immediately became friends. Paine mostly reported the anecdote by quoting the words of Doten's son:

> "They went to a little hotel at Carson, agreeing to do their work there together next morning," Doten's son said. "When morning came they set out, and suddenly on a corner Mark stopped and turned to my father, saying:
>
> "'By gracious, Alf! Isn't that a brewery?'
>
> "'It is, Mark. Let's go in.'
>
> "They did so and remained there all day, swapping yarns, sipping beer, and lunching, going back to the hotel that night.
>
> "The next morning precisely the same thing occurred. When they were on the same corner, Mark stopped as if he had never been there before, and said:

"'Good gracious, Alf! Isn't that a brewery?'

"'It is, Mark. Let's go in.'

"So again they went in, and again stayed all day.

"This happened again the next morning, and the next. Then my father became uneasy. A letter had come from Gold Hill, asking him where his report of the mines was. They agreed that next morning they would really begin the story; that they would climb to the top of a hill that overlooked the mines, and write it from there.

"But the next morning, as before, Mark was surprised to discover the brewery, and once more they went in. A few moments later, however, a man who knew all about the mines—a mining engineer connected with them—came in. He was a godsend. My father set down a valuable, informing story, while Mark got a lot of entertaining mining yarns out of him.

"Next day Virginia City and Gold Hill were gaining information from my father's article, and entertainment from Mark's story of the mines."

Much later in life, Alf Doten, in a series he called "Early Journalism of Nevada" (published in *The Nevada Magazine* in 1899), shared one of the most effective practical jokes ever pulled on Twain by the *Enterprise* staff. Doten said that the newspaper's printers decided to play the joke on the humorist when he was working at the paper with De Quille. At the time, Twain was known for perpetrating his own pranks but also for being a bad sport if he was on the receiving end.

The back-shop crew purchased a cheap knockoff of a meerschaum pipe that was as "big as a man's fist." They had a local tinsmith mount it with tin so that it resembled a genuine, silver version of the pipe and added a long, cherrywood stem and mouthpiece. As Doten recounted, "The whole rig [cost] about $2, yet [looked] to be worth about sixty."

As part of the joke, the printers persuaded De Quille to quietly tell Twain about the gift. Twain decided to reciprocate by purchasing several bottles of Champagne and some cigars, which he smuggled into the office "ready for the surprise party." That evening, the group gathered in the newsroom, and Twain was presented with the pipe. He and De Quille pretended to be surprised, with Twain giving a short speech to thank them for such a generous gift and for their appreciation of his "humble efforts" at the paper. Doten said that Twain also assured them "that this noble journalistic pipe of peace should be fondly smoked through all future generations of the Twain family, in cherished memory of this auspicious event."

With the ceremony over, Twain and De Quille produced the bottles of Champagne and cigars, and "there was much typographical and reportorial hilarity for a short time, while the wine and cigars lasted." Afterward, Twain returned to his hotel, proudly clutching the pipe.

The next day, Twain arrived at the office late and in a foul mood. Doten described him as sitting in his office chair, "with a face on him like a salivated grave-digger," and confronting De Quille:

> "See here, Dan. I've always considered you like a friend and brother, but after that infernal snide pipe affair last night I don't know. I took it home happy, and was happy all night till this morning, when I unwrapped the blamed thing and was loading it for a royal smoke, then I saw what a meersham it was. The wine and cigars cost me sixty times more than the cussed smokestack is worth, to say nothing of my chuckle-headed speech. . . . Jokes are jokes, but I don't recognize this as one."

From Good Times to Bad

In November 1867 Doten became associate editor and reporter for the *Gold Hill Daily News,* in the mining camp adjacent to Virginia City. It was during the next decade and a half, while affiliated with this newspaper (which he would own, for a time), that he achieved his most sustained financial stability. Doten hobnobbed with the Comstock's elites, including the so-called Silver Kings (John Mackay, James Fair, James Flood, and William O'Brien); and with the bankers who controlled much of the Comstock, including William Sharon and William Ralston. Nevada author Walter Van Tilburg Clark, who edited Doten's diaries into a three-volume set published in the 1970s, has referred to this time as Doten's "brief period of affluence as mining speculator and owner of the *Gold Hill Daily News,* when he is, to all intents, the big-shot he has wished to be."

His period of prosperity also included marriage. On July 24, 1873, on a steamer in the middle of Lake Tahoe, Doten married Mary Stoddard, a brilliant teacher in Gold Hill, who would eventually gain her own local fame. Stoddard, who was born in Connecticut in 1845 and who had had a brief, earlier marriage at a young age, had traveled to Virginia City in 1870 to stay with an aunt and uncle. The Dotens had four children together between 1875 and 1880.

Sadly, at the end of the 1870s, Alf Doten's economic fortunes took a dramatic turn for the worse. Due to increasing debt as a result of his unprofitable mining-stock speculation, and also because of a loss in advertising and subscription revenues during what became a permanent downturn in the local mining business, he was forced to give up ownership of the *Gold Hill Daily News,* but he remained on staff as the paper's managing editor.

He stayed at the *News* until 1881, when he left to become editor of the *Reese River Reveille* newspaper in Austin. During this same period, Mary Doten earned her Nevada certification and worked as a teacher to help keep the family financially afloat. The *Gold Hill Daily News* finally ceased publication in April 1882.

While in Austin and working for the *Reveille,* Doten also contributed a regular series of reports about that region, titled "From Eastern Nevada," to the *Enterprise.* While not outright hoaxes, a few stories that he wrote for these two papers were filled with colorful exaggeration. For example, in September 1883 he reported that one of the biggest challenges in Austin was the lack of a good sewer system. He said that the problem would be much worse if the community did not employ the use of a "peculiar scavenger bug." He described the insect as:

About the size of a dried prune, [he] has pitchfork horns, stiff, wiry legs, petrified charcoal back, no tail, and an atrocious breath. He rushes about slowly, absorbing all the domestic and foreign stinks and sewage impurities, carefully digesting and retaining the same within his internal economy, and thus rendering Austin all the more healthy. He crawls about houses, sociably and searchingly, and is quiet and inoffensive unless you disturb or injure him, when you will regret it forthwith, for he just can deliberately outstink anything else in the world. The odor of the skunk is simply bouquet fragrance in comparison.

Doten stayed at the *Reveille* until 1884 (his wife and children had moved to Reno nearly a year earlier, after she had accepted a job as one of Reno's pioneer teachers, receiving higher pay than Alf earned as an editor). He then drifted back to Virginia City, where he found work at the *Territorial Enterprise* for the next two years. For a time, he filled in for Dan De Quille, who had temporarily been fired by the paper because of his alcoholism. Doten also freelanced regularly for the *San Francisco Chronicle,* the *Reno Evening Gazette,* and *The Salt Lake Tribune.*

From 1888 to about 1895, he did whatever he could to make money, working as a carpenter, selling life insurance, writing freelance articles, and, when he could, engaging in speculation (mostly unsuccessful) on mining stocks. From about 1895 to 1899, he worked as a stringer in Carson City for the *Nevada State Journal,* covering the Nevada State Legislature, state politics, federal courts, and crime. Because the work was sporadic, he also lived on money sent weekly to him by Mary. In 1897 he joined the press throng reporting on the James Corbett and Bob Fitzsimmons heavyweight-championship fight in Carson City.

And like some of his peers, he struggled with alcohol. In 1899 Mary, who had grown increasingly unhappy with Alf's heavy drinking, banished him from the family home in Reno. Although she later relented and permitted him to return, he continued to live mostly in boardinghouses in Carson City. He also kept on writing articles whenever he could find a paying patron. He filed stories and reports with the *San Francisco Chronicle,* Reno's *Nevada State Journal,* and *The Salt Lake Tribune,* and he became a regular contributor to a new publication, *The Nevada Magazine* (not to be confused with the more modern periodical published by the state since 1936). At the turn of the century, he was hired by the US Treasury Department to write its annual report on Nevada's mining history, something he did again in some subsequent years.

According to Nevada writer Walter Van Tilburg Clark, however, in the late 1890s and early 1900s, Doten fell "from heavy but positive and social drinking into grim, unhappy alcoholism, wherein his honesty fails him, too, and he becomes completely superstitious about luck, is alienated from his family, contentiously and persistently alienates himself from his last journalistic connections, and winds up a bitter, touchy, backward-looking, panhandling, lonely old bar-fly, town drunk and figure of fun in Carson [City], occupied chiefly with dreams which would mend all, and with following closely the similar and often even more disastrous ends of other old men of his generation in the west."

On the afternoon of November 12, 1903, the writer and diarist died in his boardinghouse room in Carson City. Stories about his death noted that Doten, the man dubbed by the *Reno Evening Gazette* as the "Dean of Newspaper Men of State," had been in failing health but had appeared to be fine the prior evening when he went to bed. The *Eureka Sentinel's* obituary on November 21, 1903, said that his "body was still warm, indicating life had been extinct but a short time" when he was found. It added that Doten had suffered from "heart trouble," which was believed to be the cause of death.

The *San Francisco Call's* obituary on November 15, 1903, noted, "Aside from Mark Twain, Dan De Quille, Joe Goodman and Charles Goodwin, Alf Doten was one of the best known of the coterie of brilliant newspaper writers which at one time made the [*Territorial Enterprise*] one of the brightest papers in this country."

Despite his personal and financial problems, Doten was generally perceived in positive terms during his life and after. For example, Thompson & West *History of Nevada,* published in 1880, said, "Mr. Doten is a hearty, genial, whole-souled character that it does good to shake hands with. As an editor he is a hard worker, with logic, if wanted; with wit, if pertinent; with hard sense all the time; and sufficient caution to steer his paper safely among political reefs."

And in his book, *Editor on the Comstock,* Wells Drury wrote: "Alf Doten of the *Gold Hill Daily News* bore an honorable part in Nevada journalism. While he sought to produce a neat and workmanlike sheet, and succeeded admirably, he always recognized the primacy of news in the making of a paper."

Drury continued, "Doten was a pioneer of pioneers. And when confidential during some friendly evening talk, would draw from an inner sanctum of the office an old tin cup, battered and worn, together with a tin plate and knife and fork that had seen such use. . . . Alf had carried these relics around the Horn and through the 'gold rush' of '49."

As for his long-beleaguered wife: Mary not only taught most subjects at Reno High School and eventually served as its vice principal, but she also gained recognition as one of the state's most active suffragists. In 1895 she spoke, alongside Susan B. Anthony and Nevada educator Hannah Clapp, at the first public meeting of the state suffrage committee in Reno. Like her husband, she was also a prolific writer, contributing essays to local newspapers and writing poetry. In 1912 a new elementary school in Reno was named in her honor (it would be torn down in 1974). Mary Doten died on March 12, 1914.

9

The Vagabond

SEMBLINS says death cannot be a matter of much moment for an editor—no 30 days notice, [just] a few days as advertised on the fourth page, a few calls by subscribers not in arrears. A short, quick breath—then the subscription paper for burial expenses.

~ WILLIAM J. FORBES ~

IT'S BEEN SAID that William J. Forbes was perhaps a little too smart, a little too clever to be appreciated by his readers. Forbes, who passed through the newsrooms of nearly a dozen newspapers in Northern California and Nevada during his life, is one of the most overlooked and forgotten figures in western-frontier journalism. Admired and respected by his peers, who often reprinted his work in their own publications, Forbes had the misfortune of toiling for most of his career in remote mining camps and towns, and for publications that were often not long lived.

Although he was not technically a hoax writer like Twain, De Quille or Hart, Forbes used humor, sarcasm, and clever turns of phrase, often under his nom de plume "Semblins," to make his point. Most of his Semblins pieces were short, witty statements that caused his readers to look at a topic in a new or humorous way. Thompson & West's *History of Nevada* said of Forbes: "No member of the Nevada press was better or more widely known in his time. Some of his witty paragraphs under the nom de plume 'Semblins' became standard quotations in the United States and were repeated until their origin was lost."

Newspapers throughout the country (particularly in Nevada and California), and from nations as far away as New Zealand and Australia, picked up and reprinted the writer's Semblins pieces. Forbes capitalized on this success, writing these short articles throughout his newspaper career.

A sampling of some of the things that Semblins allegedly said over the years include:

SEMBLINS tells us of an amiable clerk who was recently pouring kerosene by candle light. Something exploded and the man was sent to Heaven without whiskers or hair—whereas a few minutes before he was happy on earth, conscious of the love of a girl with a pinback dress, and both of them having all their hair parted in the middle. Which goes to show that a man can't be too careful. A nice woman is the only proper inflammable article to fool with by candle light.

SEMBLINS asks why is it that the time of day is past 10 o'clock at 10:15, and only half past at 15 minutes later.

SEMBLINS says he doesn't want much to do with the man who puts his postage stamps on bottoms up.

SEMBLINS reads—When all the blandishment of life are gone, the coward sneaks to death—the brave live on—But the poet doesn't tell what they live on.

A SAFE PROFESSION: SEMBLINS overheard two scientific gentlemen in a private conversation. One says, "Doc, I see you have your shingle out as a regular family physician: how is that? I thought you were intending to practice the veterinary." "Well, I'll tell you, Colonel. I did practice at that, and expected to keep on it; but it's so awkward, sometimes, you know: a valuable horse dies on your hands, and there's a devilish sight of talk about it—everyone speculates upon what the horse is worth, and how he might have been saved, and there's a chance of a suit for damages—malpractice, and all that; but in this family line, if a child slips the hooks, or somebody's wife or mother-in-law dies, the ground is turned up and dug over on the whole story, and there's none of that foolish talk."

As is the case for many of his nineteenth century–Nevada newspaper brethren, details about Forbes's birthplace and early years are sketchy. He was born in 1831 in Crawford County, OH, and was the oldest child of Robert and Sarah Forbes. His father was a carpenter, and Forbes apparently learned the printing trade at a young age. He traveled west in the late 1850s or early 1860s, working at papers in Northern California mining boomtowns, such as Coloma, Marysville, and Downieville. He may or may not

have journeyed from Downieville to Nevada in 1860, in the aftermath of
the Pyramid Lake War, as part of a relief party sent to protect the citizens
of Carson City or Virginia City, who feared that the conflict might spread
to their communities.

In May 1863 he and a partner, Charles L. Perkins, packed up their printing press and hauled it over the Sierra Nevada range, from Downieville to
the Nevada mining camp of Unionville, where they started the first newspaper in Humboldt County, the weekly *Humboldt Register.*

BIRTH OF SEMBLINS

The town of Unionville welcomed Forbes and Perkins enthusiastically.
According to historians Richard Lingenfelter and Karen Rix Gash—in
The Newspapers of Nevada: A History & Bibliography, 1854–1979—the two
journalists were met with a thirty-hammer salute on an anvil and a small
parade. Lingenfelter and Gash said that the *Register* quickly became one of
the leading papers in the Nevada Territory. Forbes used its pages to begin
writing witty editorial quips or "squashes" (as the *Carson Daily Appeal* once
described them), which became known as the Semblins pieces. Within a
few months, Forbes had acquired Perkins's share in the paper.

In 1864 Forbes returned to California to marry Mary G. Mitchell in
Placerville. By then, Forbes was so well regarded by his peers that the rival
Gold Hill Daily News wrote a teasing, congratulatory note, which stated:

> Forbes, of the *Humboldt Register,* is getting young again. The alkali and
> sulphur leads of that garden spot of the world, are resuscitating the
> nature that once was in him. . . . Forbes seems to have been tempted
> by some of the Coloma fruit, and like Adam of old, was unable to
> resist the temptation, and the consequence is, that like Adam, he has
> fallen, yea, he has fallen—into the arms of one of the daughters of that
> beautiful Queen of Paradise. . . . Our editorial brother has lately been
> married.

The couple had a son, Sheridan, who was born on July 3, 1866; and a
daughter, Alice, who was born on August 15, 1868, but who died ten days
later. Although Forbes continued working in Nevada, his wife and son
apparently remained in Coloma. Sadly, she died there on October 16, 1870,
of an unreported cause.

Forbes's writing at the *Register* showed him at the top of his game. A dedicated Republican and supporter of the Union, he wrote biting commentary aimed at Unionville's Southern sympathizers, publishing such words as the following: "SEMBLINS has been watching the record of the 'superior race,' which [Confederate General Braxton] Bragg's army has made from Kentucky to Georgia. He thinks some very noble blood must *run* in the veins of Bragg's soldiers." The item reflected the fact that Bragg's Confederate troops had unsuccessfully tried to invade Kentucky in 1862, and then, after losing in several additional skirmishes against Union troops, they were forced to retreat to Georgia.

Forbes vehemently opposed Nevada's statehood efforts, saying that the territory lacked the proper infrastructure to support a state government. His editorials seemed to carry some weight, because Humboldt County rejected approval of the Nevada constitution when it came up for a statewide vote in September 1864. In one of his editorials, Forbes quite forcefully stated:

> DON'T WANT ANY CONSTITUTION—That's what's the matter. The Humboldt world is dead-set against engaging to help support any more lunk-heads till times get better. . . . If we have a State Government we'll have more fat-headed officers to support; and if we undertake to support them without taxing the mines, we'll run hopelessly into debt. If we do tax them, they'll stop the development of them.

An interesting sidenote: There were two statewide votes in the territory to approve a state constitution. The first, on January 19, 1864, was overwhelmingly rejected for a variety of technical and political reasons. The second version, which resolved those issues, was approved on September 7, 1864 (and Nevada became a state on October 31, 1864). During the months between the two votes, Forbes, joined by friends in Unionville, including future Nevada state controller William K. Parkinson and future Arizona territorial governor Anson Safford, drafted and approved their own constitution for what they called the State of Buena Vista (Unionville is located on the edge of Buena Vista Valley). Forbes's newspaper, the *Register*, closely reported on Buena Vista's first legislative session. The movement apparently died out, however, in the face of the efforts to draft and approve a second constitution for the new state of Nevada.

Forbes also was not above making fun of the state's first chief executive, territorial governor James Nye. When Nye supported state funding for construction of a sawmill and dam project on the Truckee River, and a drought caused the river to run dry before the project was completed, Forbes wrote: "Governor Nye has a dam by a mill site. But he has no mill by a damn sight."

Forbes's penchant for exaggeration and puns was particularly evident when he described the poor quality of the wood available for construction in Unionville in an 1864 column: "About half is what it is *cracked* up to be and the other half is *knot.*" He paid particular attention to the construction and building materials used for the courthouse, noting: "The courthouse is a fine place, except when it is dry and the sun [is] beating down through the thin, flat roof, or when the snow is melting and dripping through, or when rain is falling through. Happened in Tuesday during the shower and found Mr. Whitney with all the records and stationary, gathering snugly in a corner, where the rain fell no thicker than it did outside."

In an era when truth seemed subjective, Forbes could also turn gossip into sarcastic column fodder, as in this story about a recent shooting in Unionville: "No woman in this case. It grew out of a dogfight." In another instance, from July 9, 1864, Forbes dutifully reported: "An elopement took place in Santa Clara last week. Nobody hurt." When another newspaper published an article on a disaster, with the headline "DAM BROKE," he shared the item and quipped, "That's what's the matter here, though we don't commonly use such language."

THE WANDERING YEARS

In 1867 Forbes sold the *Register,* and, using the proceeds, he purchased the *Virginia Daily Union,* which he rebranded as the *Daily Trespass.* The name, he said, reflected his act of trespassing in a market already occupied by several other newspapers. Published every evening, except on Sunday, the *Trespass* was well written and respected but not, ultimately, a financial success. In October 1868 a discouraged Forbes discontinued the paper and relocated to the booming mining camps of White Pine County, where he opened a saloon and soon assumed control of the *White Pine News,* moving it from Treasure City to Hamilton, which was then the seat of the county.

While operating the *News,* Forbes engaged in a bitter circulation battle with a rival newspaper, the *Inland Empire.* The two papers traded barbs over who had the largest circulation and the most advertisers, with Forbes accusing the *Empire's* editors of being "willful falsifiers" who violated the basic code of respectable journalism. Ultimately Forbes prevailed, and the *Empire* ceased publication, but the victory came as White Pine district mines were in decline. Forbes cut the *News* down to weekly publication in November 1872, then sold it in February 1873.

Forbes launched his next news effort in the tiny, eastern-Nevada mining town of Schellbourne, which had originally been established as a military outpost to provide protection for Pony Express riders and Butterfield Overland Mail stagecoaches. In the 1870s, following nearby gold discoveries, it experienced a brief boom. In September 1873 Forbes was in Schellbourne and announced plans to start the *Schell Creek Prospect* newspaper. The project, however, never came to fruition, and Forbes told the *Eureka Sentinel* that he was instead considering the idea of starting a paper in Battle Mountain, which he planned to call the *Battle Mountain Thunderer.*

The peripatetic Forbes, however, next showed up in the central Nevada mining-boomtown of Eureka, where, in March 1874, he established yet another newspaper with an unusual name (an ongoing quirk), the *Cupel.* Wells Drury said that the name was significant to the local populace because:

Eureka was a camp in which all the ores required smelting, and in order to make a test the assayer was compelled to make use of the cupel, a little receptacle of bone-ash in which the precious metals, mixed with base metals, were placed and subjected to a high degree of heat. The cupel absorbed or eliminated the base metals, leaving on top a shining button of pure gold and silver, ready for weighing and showing accurately the value of the ore. It would be difficult to select a name more appropriate for a true newspaper—one that fills the requirements of the profession, which is in honor bound to show forth the precious metals of truth and justice and to cast away the baser admixtures of prejudice, bias and misrepresentation.

Sadly, like many of his other ventures, the *Cupel* was not a success and would collapse after only four months. On July 24, 1874, torrential rains caused a literal wall of water to sweep down Eureka Canyon, demolishing nearly every building in the town. The *Cupel's* offices, along with most other buildings in the path of the raging water, were swept away.

Following his unfortunate experiences in eastern and central Nevada, Forbes moved on to Salt Lake City, where he established a Gentile (non-Mormon) newspaper, the *New Endowment.* Like all of Forbes's publications, the paper was attractive and well written—even the Latter-day Saints' *Millennial Star* publication in 1873 described it in a complimentary way: "Its articles, as far as we can judge from casual perusal, evince considerable literary ability."

But despite Forbes's best efforts, the *Endowment* also ended in failure. In July 1873 the *Eureka Sentinel* published a short article titled, simply, "No More," which said: "The [Salt Lake] *New Endowment* is no more. It appeared for the last time on the 8th of the month. We are truly sorry that Brother Forbes could not make it stick." A few years later, in 1875, the *Territorial Enterprise* called it "an unfortunate venture, which absorbed all of his [Forbes's] remaining means and well-nigh broke his heart."

Forbes's own editorial take on the paper's demise was direct, as usual: "This is the last number of the *New Endowment*. For what in its time it has been, it has existence credit to the undersigned. For its shortcomings, the same tracings are good. Everybody whose appreciation I care for like The Paper now. I would like to publish it longer on that account; but the fact is, I did not bring enough money."

After his failed effort in Utah, Forbes returned to Nevada in the winter of 1873 and followed through on his earlier musings about starting a paper in Battle Mountain. Motivated by his love of unusual and pertinent names, he called the publication *Measure for Measure,* which alludes to a play by Shakespeare with the same title and to a Bible verse, Matthew 7:2: "For with what judgment you judge, you will be judged; and with the measure you use, it will be measured back to you."

For the next two years, Forbes single-handedly produced the weekly newspaper. He continued to write all of the "locals," or news briefs, and he even gave a shout-out to one of his fellow editors, writing: "Fred Hart, the very popular local and correspondent of the *Reese River Reveille,* passed through the other day. Fred is a good boy—and becoming better every day."

As was true at any frontier newspaper, the job was not without some occasional risks. For example, the *Eureka Sentinel* reported that on December 3, 1874, "W. J. Forbes was struck on the head with a pistol at Battle Mountain, last Saturday night. So far we have been unable to ascertain the particulars, as our informant did not know of the person who struck the blow, or why it was struck."

The strain involved in selling advertising and subscriptions, writing all the stories, setting all the type, and hand-printing all the copies—and in getting pistol-whipped—took a toll on the veteran newspaperman. While he had always enjoyed imbibing, Forbes began drinking more heavily, which began to impact his overall health.

On the morning of October 30, 1875, a friend stopped by Forbes's cabin and found him dead in his bed. Reports at the time said that he had "retired last night early in apparent good health." The cause was listed as "disease of the heart," which may have been true in more ways than the obvious one. Forbes was buried in Coloma beside the graves of his wife and daughter. His son, Sheridan, died in 1914 and was buried nearby.

Wells Drury later wrote that Forbes "was bright with the undeniable brightness of unquenchable genius." He continued:

> Old timers still laugh about his quips and fancies. Writing under the pen-name of "Semblins," he touched on every subject known to man, and his shafts so often hit the mark that he became popular with all classes of readers.
>
> This man simply could not keep out of a printing office. Journalism was his natural element. Quick at repartee, trained in the use of a rich and variegated vocabular that contained every known expression of disapprobation, his bitter words often left scars that were slow to heal. . . . He had fought a fight against all odds all his life, was one of the brightest geniuses the coast had ever seen, but he lacked the faculty of making and saving money and lived in communities where his mental superiority was more envied than appreciated.

His obituary in the *Arizona Weekly Journal-Miner* mentioned that Forbes "was well known as a witty and crisp writer, having gained quite a reputation in that line," while an obit in the *Territorial Enterprise* said, "A strangely eccentric and gifted soul fled when he died." After describing his many accomplishments, the *Enterprise* noted that he had been publishing *Measure for Measure* in Battle Mountain for the previous two years and that "it [had] been evident that the bright genius was waning, and the news of his death will bring no surprise." The paper continued:

> Forbes was full of strange contradiction. He was never a man of culture, but he could say things sometimes which set the whole Coast laughing. His wit was sometimes inclined to be coarse, but it was inimitable of its kind. He could twist more strange, unexpected and comical meanings out of a few words than any man alive. His sense of humor

and the ridiculous was infinite, and it was his wont to convulse his listeners with quaint expressions which no one but Forbes would ever have thought of.

His ways were often cold and distant to strangers, but his friendships were very strong, and in his dealings with his fellowmen his integrity was never questioned. His life is cut down in its prime, and it is simply duty in closing this hasty sketch to say that a convivial habit, acquired among the wild spirits which filled the Sierras in the old flush days, increased upon him, until at last it undermined his health and usefulness and brought him to a premature grave. May all that was right and good in his life be treasured, and may all his weaknesses be hid with him in the sepulcher.

10

The Major

A lie once told travels with the speed of a winged Mercury.

~ MAJOR JOHN H. DENNIS ~

For most of his long newspaper career, John Hancock Dennis was what you might call a straight-news writer. Certainly, he engaged in friendly sparring in print with his contemporaries at other newspapers, particularly with rivals in Carson City and Eureka. He shared homey aphorisms in his editorial columns, but he was not a committed hoax writer like Mark Twain or Dan De Quille. He also was a remarkably successful politician who served in the California State Assembly and in the Nevada State Senate, representing Elko County, NV, from 1882 to 1886; and who served as an elector in two presidential votes and as sheriff, county clerk, and county commissioner in Lander County, NV.

Dennis, who would eventually work at eight or more newspapers in Nevada, Utah, and California, was born in Concord, MA, on May 28, 1835, and he attended public schools in the Concord area before graduating from Boston High School. In 1852 he struck out for California to make his fortune, sailing around South America's Cape Horn on his journey to get there. Alfred Doten wrote that he had first encountered Dennis in 1854 when they were both working in the gold-placer diggings in California's Amador County. After failing to get rich during the gold rush, Dennis found work as a reporter with the *San Francisco Herald* and, from 1860 to 1862, served a single term in the California State Assembly, representing El Dorado County. He also became editor of the *Eldorado Times* in Placerville, CA.

That "Major" Title

In 1871 Dennis relocated to Nevada to become editor and co-owner of Austin's *Reese River Reveille*. In addition to his newspaper duties, Dennis found time to serve in several political roles in Lander County, including as county clerk and as a county commissioner. He sold his stake in the paper three years later and became editor and co-owner of the *Eureka Sentinel.*

It was during his time in Eureka that Dennis earned the title "Major" by which he was known for the rest of his life. The story behind how he received this military honor is as follows:

In 1875 a Goshute Native American named Toby promised to lead two white men, James Toland and Albert Leathers, to the location of a potentially valuable mining lode in the Spring Valley area of eastern Nevada. In return, the men would pay Toby fifty dollars. Apparently, after being shown the site, the white men refused to pay, saying that there was no ore there. In response, Toby is said to have killed Toland, but Leathers escaped and made his way to the Cleveland Ranch in Spring Valley, the most successful ranch in the area.

Leathers claimed that the Goshutes were on the rampage, and in response, ranch owner Abner C. Cleveland gathered some of his hands and set out with them to find Toland's body. Along the way, they encountered a Goshute man who resisted arrest, and they killed him. The next day they shot and killed another Goshute, who was out hunting and who refused to give up his rifle to the armed posse. The group also killed a third Native American, who they thought was heading into the area to join the alleged attack by the Native Americans.

While this was occurring, a large number of Goshutes had already gathered in Spring Valley for their annual fall pine-nut harvest. When word spread of the murders, the group became concerned about an attack from the local white population. Concurrently, the presence of so many Goshutes worried local white settlers, who misunderstood why the Native Americans were in Spring Valley and who thought that the tribe was planning to retaliate for the killings. Several newspapers, including the *Pioche Daily Record,* published alarmist stories, with the *Daily Record* announcing that "All Indians in Eastern Nevada are on the Warpath."

Cleveland requested military help from Nevada governor Lewis D. Bradley, who, in turn, asked US military troops stationed in San Francisco to help quell the alleged uprising. However, General John M. Schofield, commander of the far western forces, had serious doubts about the claims and ordered a small company of nine men at Fort Halleck in Elko County to travel to White Pine County, "not to make war nor to punish anybody but to preserve the peace."

A group of about fifty white ranchers coalesced at Absalom Lehman's ranch (now part of Great Basin National Park), located in the adjacent Snake Valley, to seek justice. The Goshutes, eager to avoid escalating the conflict, agreed to turn Toby over to the US troops for a trial. Unfortunately, the ranchers, who vastly outnumbered the troops, wanted immediate justice and demanded that Toby be turned over to them. Not wanting to engage with the ranchers, the troops complied, and the Goshute was hanged on the spot.

While this was happening, Dennis, who was a good friend of Governor Bradley, organized a volunteer militia in Eureka and traveled to Abner Cleveland's ranch. He was given the title Major as the militia's leader. Dennis's forces were never actually called into battle, but their presence helped persuade both the ranchers and the Native Americans to ease the tensions finally, and the matter was quickly resolved.

The Time Two Women Fell in Love

In 1877 Dennis sold his Eureka holdings and moved on to become editor and co-owner of Tuscarora's *Mining Review* newspaper, which immediately merged with another local paper, the *Tuscarora Times*, becoming the *Tuscarora Times-Review*. Dennis would have a lengthy association with the newspaper, serving as editor twice, from 1877 to 1881 and again from 1883 to 1886 (he briefly worked as editor of the *Salt Lake City Democrat* in 1882). While working at the *Times-Review*, he wrote and published a series of articles titled "Female Husband" in 1878, a straight-news account about a marriage between two women, something considered scandalous at the time.

Dennis's articles focused on a story that began in 1878, when sixteen-year-old Marancy Hughes came forward to say that her marriage six months earlier to Samuel Pollard in Tuscarora was a sham, because Pollard was really a woman named Sarah. Hughes said that Pollard had been working as a silver miner in a local mine when the two had met and had fallen in love and, over the objections of her uncle and guardian, had eloped on September 29, 1877. The marriage had seemed fine for the next few months until Hughes returned to her uncle's home and revealed that her husband was a woman in disguise. She said that on the night of their marriage, Pollard had revealed her secret and had told Hughes that she (Pollard) had gotten into some trouble in Colorado and had assumed the guise of a man. The newspaper also said Hughes alleged that Pollard had threatened to kill her if she ever shared the truth.

In response, the uncle, J. C. Howerton, filed a formal complaint accusing Pollard of perjury for having claimed that she was a man on the marriage license. The story took an intriguing twist once Pollard was taken into custody. Apparently, on the day of the trial, Hughes encountered Pollard for the first time since she had fled and, in the words of the *Winnemucca Silver Star,* "immediately threw her arms around the neck of Pollard, whom she fondly kissed and in the wildest excitement begged that she might be permitted to remain there and not be sent back to the house of her relatives, saying that she desired to remain with her husband and never wanted to leave him any more."

The wish was granted by the court, and the two went off to have dinner in a nearby restaurant, while a police officer constrained Hughes's grandmother, who sought to confront the two. For the next two years, Pollard and Hughes remained together, with the former even conducting a regional lecture tour, during which she appeared as a man in the first half, then as a woman in the second portion. However, the strain of having so much attention on their relationship apparently became too great, and the two separated for good in 1880.

"A Few 'Sticksful' of Fiction"
Despite his inclination to write about such subjects as the "Female Husband" with a straight-news approach, Dennis decided, a few years later, to have some fun with his readers at the *Tuscarora Times-Review.* In 1884, on a slow news day, he wrote and published "A Luminous Tree," a joke with unintended consequences. Two decades later, he explained what had happened:

> Sometime in the early eighties when this writer was engineer-in-chief of the *Tuscarora Times-Review,* one afternoon when the insatiable "comps" [composing room staff] were hustling him for copy to fill a small "hole" in the local column he gave rein to his imagination and hurriedly dashed off a few "sticksful" of fiction relative to an alleged luminous tree or bush, which he located at an indefinite distance and in an indefinite direction from the town of Tuscarora.
>
> He had no more idea of deceiving anybody than had the author of the Arabian Nights in his relation of the wonderous tale of Sharazada [Scheherazade]. What, then, was his surprise, mortification, and grief when his little "flyer" commenced to be copied as truth in the papers in the East and Europe and letters began pouring in with a request for

further information and specimens of this wondrous foliage from all points of the compass, with several inquiries from tourists as to facilities for transportation, hotel accommodations, etc. in the vicinity of this wondrous specimen of phosphorescent forestry. The unfortunate pencil pusher fruitlessly endeavored to ease his conscience and terminate his annoyance by publishing a supplemental item to the effect that the luminous tree had been destroyed by superstitious [Native Americans] and that all signs of its existence had been obliterated, but the item fell still-born. . .the experience of the writer should prove a warning to little boys and girls never to tell a fib, even in fun.

Dennis added that the lie had refused to go away, despite his attempts to set the record straight, and that he had been further dismayed several years later when an Ohio scientist included the supposed existence of the luminous tree in a book titled *Geographical Spice*.

So, what was this story, which Dennis considered to be such a blemish on his hard-earned reputation? On July 31, 1884, he penned the following completely invented item:

Near Tuscarora, Nevada, grows a tree which the Indians call the "witch tree," because it sends out a phosphorescent light which is so great that it can be seen a mile away in a dark night. A person standing near can see to read the finest print. Its foliage resembles that of the bay tree of California. Its luminous property is caused by a gummy substance which covers its branches. This is thought to be a parasitic growth, and can be rubbed off with the hand. The tree grows to a height of six or seven feet, with a trunk six or eight inches in diameter. The Indians will never approach the tree even in the daytime.

Twain and De Quille would have been proud.

Looking back on this journalistic misadventure, Dennis said that what particularly perplexed him was the fact that the luminous tree hoax had continued to spread, even years after he had attempted to put the story to rest. And yet his stories about the two women—which happened to be true—hadn't nowhere near the same reach or longevity:

As an instance of human credulity and incredulity, the "Luminous Tree" fake and the "Female Husband" sensations, which were detailed in the *Times-Review* about the same time, are striking instances. In the relation of the former there is not a word of truth, and no person of ordinary common sense was expected to believe it. The latter was not only founded on fact, but every word published in relation thereto was unembellished truth. And yet the incredible tale passed current, while the truthful one was almost universally regarded as a hoax. Verily, truth is stranger than fiction, and we fear in this simple world—considerably scarcer.

Coming into His Own

In the early 1880s Dennis also tried his hand at writing a play, crafting a now-lost work called *The Red Roarers of Tuscarora.* Apparently written as a holiday play, it was "a tale of love and crime unequaled for strong dramatic situation and tearful pathos."

As his career progressed, he was not immune to the playful sparring that often occurred between newspaper editors at the time. In the late 1880s, Dennis and the editors of the *Carson Daily Appeal* traded quips about each other in the pages of their respective newspapers. For example, in 1886, under the headline "A Queer Mistake," the *Appeal* wrote:

> John Dennis is one of the most unfortunate editors in the State, and although meaning well at times, occasionally gets into some terrible situations.
>
> A few days ago, he wrote these two items:
>
> "The citizens of Tuscarora are mourning the loss of twenty valuable dogs, poisoned by some miscreant."
>
> "The butchers, Sayles & Bayley, announce that they have just made up a large batch of fine, large sausages."
>
> These two items, by the devilish ingenuity of the foreman, appeared one under the other, and Sayles took it as a personal reflection and came in and knocked the unfortunate editor off a stool.

Dennis also shared the occasional clever aphorism in his editorial pages, which, much like William Forbes's Semblins items, was designed to offer a bit of whimsy to the newspaper. A couple examples are as follows:

> It seems as if all the workers in both hemispheres were either striking or being thrown out of employment. But there is one laborer who seldom strikes. It is the patient wife and mother, the shift-boss of the

family, who cooks, scrubs and delves, while her old man takes things easy.

It is against the law to sell meat in San Francisco on Sunday. But there is no trouble in getting as full of whiskey as a goose.

Politics Comes Calling

In 1882 Dennis was elected a Nevada state senator, representing Elko County, and he served for four years. He was so well respected that in 1885, some newspapers thought that he should make himself available as a candidate for governor. In May of that year, the *Carson Daily Appeal* opined: "There is talk among the Democrats, of nominating John Dennis for Governor, as he is looked upon as the most available man in the party. His long career in this State as a journalist and politician has been an honorable and able one, and his record is not tainted with jobbery of any description." The talk, however, apparently never amounted to much because Dennis never ran for governor.

From 1884 to 1889, Dennis also worked in Battle Mountain, where he edited the short-lived *Battle Mountain Messenger* (in 1884) and later was co-owner and editor of the *Central Nevadan* (from 1884 to 1889). Following his time in the Nevada legislature, he was hired to oversee the Melter & Refiner operations at the US Mint in Carson City. The office was tasked with taking bullion delivered to the mint and turning it into silver and gold ingots. The ingots were then sent to the coiners office, where they were rolled into strips and then cut into blank rounds that were pressed into coins.

After four years in that position, Dennis returned to Austin to edit the *Reese River Reveille* for two years. Next, he joined the staff of the *Virginia City Chronicle* in 1893 and wrote freelance stories for the *Reno Evening Gazette*. At the same time, he continued to play an important role in statewide politics, serving first as a presidential elector representing the Nevada Democratic Party in 1880 and then as an elector representing the Silver-Democrats in 1900.

It was while working as a legislative correspondent for the *Gazette* in 1895 that Dennis used a pen name—"Joblots"—for the only time in his long career. He covered a wide array of legislative stories, including a Purity of Elections bill, so perhaps the use of a nom de plume permitted him to write more freely. As Joblots, he wrote that the bill had passed the state senate "by the Heavenly majority of eleven to three," and he added, "I am too happy for utterance or writerance [*sic*]. Farewell, a long farewell to the potency of the sack, and all hail to the blessed era of decent politics in the battle born commonwealth of Nevada. Bless the Seventeenth session, with all of its short comings. Praise God from whom all blessings flow."

From 1901 to 1904, Dennis reached perhaps the pinnacle of his long journalism career in Nevada when he was named editor of the *Nevada State Journal,* one of the largest newspapers in the state at the time. He retired in 1904, however, due to declining health. In May 1906 the *Carson Daily Appeal* reported, in rather blunt fashion, that Dennis, who was staying with a friend in the capital city, was in "very poor health. . .acute bronchial catarrh is the cause of his present illness and he fully understands that it is only a question of time and not many months either when he will have passed away."

The article said that he was "wasted to a shadow and weighs less than one hundred pounds," but added, "the inroads of disease has in no way affected his vigorous intellect or dampened his splendid courage. He is the same John Dennis as of yore, his conversation is as sprightly as ever and he is game as a grey wolf in the face of fate."

Speaking for himself, Dennis told the *Appeal* writer:

> I don't want any one coming in here to tell me I am looking better and will be up all right in time to vote at the fall elections. I know better than that and I know perfectly well the end is not far off and I am quite ready for it. I don't want any sympathy from any one. I like my friends to drop in and tell some good stories and no one need tread lightly on the floor or look grave. I have no troubles of conscience for my past life for I don't recall any one that I have wronged and I don't fear the future state. I have fought the fight and finished the course and been a good Democrat.

Following a long illness, Dennis, who never married, died on March 21, 1907, in Reno. He was buried in the Lone Mountain Cemetery in Carson City. In recognition of Dennis's legislative service, Governor John Sparks sent a formal letter to legislators on that same day, informing them about the journalist's death and noting, "[The] Deceased was among the most prominent journalists, politicians, and public men in the history of this state, at one time a State Senator, and filled several Federal offices with honor and dignity to the State, and credit to himself. By his death, the State has suffered the loss of a distinguished citizen, an efficient and faithful officer." In response, the State Assembly approved a resolution of regret and an expression of honor on his behalf.

Wells Drury described Dennis as "a trenchant, fearless writer [who] possessed a vitriolic and witty pen that made him a terror to his contemporaries. He was a natural politician and for several sessions represented Lander [County] in the upper house of the State Legislature. His speeches were of the fiery, sledgehammer order and he could hold his own in debate with any one he ever met in the Senate. In his leisure moments he would concoct hoaxes that would go the rounds. One of the most conspicuous was his fictitious account of a 'Luminous Shrub' that grew near Tuscarora. It was discussed all over the Union, and several eastern botanists came to Nevada to investigate it."

In September 1913, a few years after Dennis's death, Sam Davis's *Carson Daily Appeal* printed a look back at Dennis's career, calling him "a remarkable man and when he ran the *Tuscarora Times-Review* it was copied all over the Union." The story also shared an anecdote—repeated by several of Dennis's peers over the years—regarding a fight that he allegedly was involved in while he was living in Austin. Apparently, Dennis and another man disagreed vehemently about how an election was being conducted and began to fight in front of the polling place. Both men were arrested and were parked in the city jail. Dennis was able to pay bail to get out, but the other man was broke. As Dennis was leaving, the other man said that if Dennis would pay his bail as well, he would agree to finish the fight. Dennis paid the forty-dollar bail, and the two agreed to resume their fight in a ravine outside of town to avoid the authorities. According to the *Appeal* story, "To make a long story short, the man Dennis bailed out was in bed a week."

11

The Editors

Editors, like other shrewd men, must live with their eyes open.

~ attributed to A.D. JONES, editor of the *Pioche Daily Record* ~

A NYONE WHO HAS ever worked at a newspaper knows that reporters don't get to decide exactly what is published. Reporters generally don't write the headlines—although they can suggest them—and don't have the final say on what is or is not included in a story. Typically, there are individuals above the reporters who are responsible for those decisions: the editors.

So, in order for a clever hoax or a fake-news story to actually make its way into print, it must be vetted and approved by one of those editors—unless, as was the case with many small, frontier newspapers, the editor is not only the owner or co-owner but is also the primary reporter and can publish whatever they want. Thus, without the support of an editor or owner, Twain doesn't get to petrify a man or kill an entire family, and De Quille can't make rocks sing or have them move mysteriously, nor can he discover eyeless fish and underwater passageways.

A GOOD MAN

Perhaps no editor and owner permitted as much journalistic creativity as Joseph T. Goodman did. He co-owned and eventually outright owned the *Territorial Enterprise* from 1861 to 1874. Prior to his arrival, the newspaper saw a rapid changing of the guard in its early years. William L. Jernegan and Alfred James founded the newspaper in Genoa in December 1858. In August 1859 James sold his interest to Jonathan Williams, who relocated the paper to Carson City just three months later. In October 1860 Williams, who had become the sole proprietor, moved it to Virginia City.

In 1863 Goodman and Denis McCarthy gained ownership of the *Enterprise,* and, in 1865, McCarthy, who had handled the print side while

Goodman had overseen the editorial side, sold his share to Goodman, who finally became the sole owner. Under Goodman's guidance, the *Enterprise* became larger, with more pages than any of the newspapers published at that time in San Francisco. In Berkove's words, "Goodman. . .ran the paper so successfully that its sales made it independent of both government and big business. Without being 'reformist,' the paper nevertheless stood for honest government and political principle, and Goodman set the tone."

The paper also became a creative hub for young journalists under Goodman's careful guidance. Charles C. Goodwin (often referred to as Judge Goodwin), who eventually joined the *Enterprise* staff in 1873 and who then served as the *Enterprise*'s chief editor from 1875 to 1880, after Goodman had sold the paper, later wrote that Goodman had provided a "steadying influence" over the staff, offering particular mentorship to the young Mark Twain.

"I think Mark Twain out of pure gratitude to him should have left him part of his fortune," Goodwin said. "Goodman himself is as brave a man as ever lived, a thorough journalist, with magnificent journalistic judgement, and he steadied Mark through the years and was Mark's particular inspiration."

Similarly, Alf Doten, who competed against Goodman's *Enterprise*, had nothing but praise for Goodman's editorial talents: "Joseph Goodman was a brilliant and logical as well as a critical editor, and as a true poet he had few superiors, as attested by many a poetic gem from his facile pen, published in the columns of the old *Enterprise*. The only Nevada editor who ever got rich, retired rich and stays rich was Joe Goodman of the old *Enterprise*. He was the early bird who got the fat worm."

A modest man, Goodman always declined to take full credit for "discovering" Mark Twain or for establishing the creative incubator known as the *Enterprise*, through which so many talented writers and editors passed.

Joseph Thompson Goodman was born in Masonville, NY, on September 18, 1838, and moved to California with his father when he was eighteen years old. He obtained work as a typesetter at the *Golden Era*, where so many noteworthy Comstock journalists got their start. It was also where Goodman became acquainted with Denis McCarthy, his future partner at the *Territorial Enterprise*, and with Rollin M. Daggett, who owned the *Golden Era* and who would also become an *Enterprise* editor.

In 1863, when Goodman and McCarthy took over the *Enterprise*, Virginia City was in full bloom as one of the most notable, bustling communities in the western United States. Local mines were producing at high levels, and new construction was occurring all over town, including

St. Paul's Episcopal Church and the original Piper's Opera House. The booming community was a melting pot of ethnicities, drawing miners from all over America, Europe, and China.

Soon after gaining control of the paper, Goodman and McCarthy began to hire a sort of "murderers' row" of talented western journalists, starting with De Quille and continuing with Twain, Townsend, Daggett, Doten, Goodwin, and other promising writers. In addition to having a keen eye for talent and a steady editorial hand, Goodman was himself a gifted writer, excelling as an editorialist, poet (newspapers frequently published poetry at that time), and play reviewer for the *Enterprise*. De Quille noted that during Goodman's time as editor-in-chief of the *Enterprise*, he "did all the work except the local [news]."

Arthur McEwen, a well-respected reporter at the rival *Virginia City Evening Chronicle* in the 1870s, who later became managing editor of the *San Francisco Examiner* and chief editorial writer for the *New York American*, described Goodman as:

> A young man of distinct gifts. A poet of imagination, a scholar, a dramatic critic, a playwright and a writer of leaders that had the charm of entire freedom from every restriction save his own judgement of what ought not to be said. Everything from his pen possessed the literary quality. Original, forcible, confident, mocking and alive with the impulses of an abounding and generous youth, the Enterprise was to Goodman a safety-valve for his ideas rather than a daily burden of responsibility.

Similarly, Wells Drury, who served as city and managing editor of the *Enterprise* after Goodman sold the paper, wrote that Goodman was a "commanding figure in Nevada journalism" who "did more to form the high spirit of the press in that region than any other man of the profession."

During his thirteen years guiding the *Enterprise*, Goodman was a benevolent overseer who, in Berkove's words, "was a bold spirit, self-confident, exceptionally talented and able, and a paragon of integrity and courage." He provided his gifted staff with the freedom and encouragement to be creative and backed them even when their hoaxes or pranks were not well received. While he did not directly engage in the type of hoaxes concocted by Twain and De Quille, he was a willing participant in some of the many pranks perpetrated by his staff.

One of the most famous actually occurred in 1866, after Twain had left the *Enterprise* and had returned to Virginia City while on a lecture tour. Twain's official biographer, Albert Bigelow Paine, recounted that Twain's lecture had sold out and that the humorist was being urged to schedule a second appearance to allow more people to hear his talk. In response, he said that he couldn't bring himself to "give it twice in the same town."

Paine claimed that several of Twain's old friends, led by his former roommate and close friend Steve Gillis—a typesetter at the *Enterprise*—concocted a scheme to pretend to rob Twain about a week after his lecture in Gold Hill. Gillis, who made a "death bed" confession about the episode to Paine in 1907, said that a group of Twain's friends, wearing black masks, had waited at the Divide (the largely uninhabited land separating Gold Hill and Virginia City) for Twain, who was accompanied by McCarthy, another friend in on the joke.

The masked men pointed their firearms at Twain and demanded that he turn over his watch and a carpetbag filled with the proceeds from his lecture. In Paine's account, Twain wasn't scared and talked to the robbers "in his regular fashion." Paine wrote that the men, after robbing Twain of his watch, money, keys, and pencils, told Twain and McCarthy to stand there for fifteen minutes with their hands up.

A short time later, as Paine recounted, Twain and McCarthy then met up with Gillis and the other co-conspirators at a Virginia City saloon, and, after hearing about the robbery, Gillis gave Twain one hundred dollars from the humorist's own money, so that he could buy a round of drinks for the group. Gillis said that someone in the group pointed out to Twain that he would have to give another lecture now, which was immediately scheduled, and suggested that the robbery would be a great subject.

Unfortunately for Gillis and the others, one of the men who was in on the joke had been unable to keep it secret and had told Twain about the scheme the night before. After the phony holdup, while playing cards with Joseph Goodman (who was also in on the prank and who was safeguarding the stolen wares), Twain revealed that he had known about the fake robbery in advance but that he planned to have every one of the participants arrested.

"He said it with such solemn gravity, and such vindictiveness that I believed he was in dead earnest," Goodman is quoted as saying. In the end, Goodman returned Twain's watch, keys, and money and begged him not to have his friends arrested. Twain eventually relented, saying, "Well, Joe;

I'll let this pass—this time; I'll forgive them again; I've had to do it so many times; but if I should see Denis McCarthy and Steve Gillis mounting the scaffold to-morrow, and I could save them by turning over my hand, I wouldn't do it!"

The following day, Twain canceled the additional lecture, and, as he headed off in the stagecoach that would take him to his next stop in California, he reportedly stuck his head out a window, with a big smile on his face, and yelled, "Good-by; friends; Good-by thieves; I bear you no malice."

Goodman largely remained friendly with but independent of Nevada's railroad and mining interests during his ownership of the *Enterprise,* although he occasionally used the newspaper's pages to criticize key figures in these industries. *However,* in 1874 he decided to sell the paper to William Sharon, co-owner of the Virginia & Truckee Railroad and also Nevada's representative for the powerful Bank of California, which held many of the area's mines and reduction mills. Goodman, during the 1872 election—in which Sharon had unsuccessfully sought one of Nevada's two US Senate seats—had published several editorials and articles critical of the businessman and had undoubtedly played an important role in Sharon's loss. But when the state's other US Senate seat opened up two years later, Sharon effectively neutralized the *Enterprise*'s influence by buying the paper for $50,000, reportedly five times its worth.

Following the sale of the paper, Goodman and his family relocated to California. He spent several years working at various newspapers in the Golden State, dabbled (mostly unsuccessfully) in the stock market in San Francisco, and, for a time, owned and operated a raisin farm in Fresno. In 1884 he founded a literary publication in San Francisco, the *San Franciscan,* and sold it six months later. It was during this time that Goodman began to pursue another interest: studying and deciphering the Maya calendar.

Writing in the October–December 1919 issue of *American Anthropologist* magazine, famed archaeologist Sylvanus Griswold Morley noted: "Although Mr. Goodman was more widely known through his literary and journalistic activities, especially in California, it is rather through his fundamental contributions to the decipherment of the Maya hieroglyphic writing that he will be remembered by the readers of the *American Anthropologist,* contributions indeed which have won for him in this complex field of investigation unique distinction as the American Champollion [Jacque Champollion was a French scholar, who was the first to figure out how to decipher ancient Egyptian hieroglyphics]."

In 1892 Goodman and his family then moved to Alameda, CA, where he would reside for the remainder of his life. He continued working on his Maya calendar research, authoring a book titled *Archaic Maya Inscriptions,* which was published in England in 1897 and was considered the definitive work on the subject for many years. He also penned several well-received poems, including "Virginia City"; wrote his best-known short story, "The Trumpet Comes to Pickeye"; and wrote several articles reminiscing about the Comstock newspaper crowd. In addition, he continued regularly corresponding with Twain, something he had done since the latter departed Virginia City in 1864.

After being in ill-health for several months, Goodman died in San Francisco's German Hospital on October 2, 1917, at the age of 80.

ROLLIN M. DAGGETT

A sometime rival of Goodman's—and another longtime *Enterprise* editor of note—Rollin M. Daggett joined the newspaper staff as a reporter in 1862 and served as Goodman's associate editor, before succeeding him as editor-in-chief in 1874, shortly after Goodman sold the paper. Daggett and Goodman got to know each other well when the latter worked on Daggett's *Golden Era* literary weekly in San Francisco. Although they became good friends, the two news editors also became rivals when it came to writing long, commemorative poems to mark national holidays, special celebrations, or the death of a notable person. About once each week, a poem by Goodman or Daggett would appear in the *Enterprise,* and they would take turns gloating over their own work's reception by the public. The two also collaborated on several plays, including *The Psychoscope: A Sensational Drama in Five Acts,* which premiered at Piper's Opera House in Virginia City.

While Daggett was never Twain's editor, he worked alongside him, and he did serve as De Quille's editor for several years. Francis Phelps Weisenburger, author of *Idol of the West: The Fabulous Career of Rollin Mallory Daggett,* noted, "Clemens [Twain] developed a close association with Daggett. . . . Daggett became one of Clemens' 'staunchest friends.' It was Daggett who introduced him around the *Enterprise* office."

Describing Daggett in Sam Davis's *History of Nevada,* Wells Drury wrote:

> Rollin M. Daggett dearly loved a fight. The roar of battle was music to his ears. The smell of burning powder was incense to his nostrils.

"The thunder of the captains and the shouting" delighted his intrepid soul. He was ever eager for the fray, and never lowered his lance in the presence of an enemy. Yet, in moments of peace, he was as gentle as a dove. So strangely were the qualities mixed in him that while his foes dreaded him for his incisive, vitriolic excoriations, his friends loved him for his warm heart and his charming manners.

Daggett, who was born in Richville, NY, on February 22, 1831, moved with his family to Defiance, OH, in 1837. While living there, he was educated in local schools and learned the printing business. In 1850 he traveled west, much of it on foot, and spent the next two years prospecting in Northern California, earning enough money to embark on his next adventure. He relocated to San Francisco in 1852, where he first worked as a printer and then began publishing the *Golden Era*. Eight years later, he sold his interest in the publication and partnered with several newsmen to establish the *San Francisco Daily Evening Mirror*, a news and literary paper.

In 1862, after the *Mirror* had merged with the rival *Daily Herald*, Daggett decided to seek greener pastures and traveled to booming Virginia City, where he established a brokerage house and became active in territorial politics. This is also when he joined the reportorial staff of the *Territorial Enterprise* as a part-timer. During this period, the staff largely consisted of young, unmarried men in their twenties and thirties, and they were prone to pranking and teasing, smoking cigars, staying out late in local saloons, and generally living a bachelor lifestyle. Weisenburger described the newspaper office as "like that of a fraternity house without a house mother."

Much later, in 1878, toward the end of his tenure as the *Enterprise's* editor, Daggett became embroiled in a spat with noted New York journalist and editor Mrs. Miriam Leslie, who was married to Frank Leslie, publisher of the nationally renowned *Frank Leslie's Illustrated Newspaper*. After visiting Virginia City as part of research for a cross-country travel book, Mrs. Leslie had written that the community was a "'Godforsaken' town where an innocent evening walk required a police escort."

In response, Daggett attacked Mrs. Leslie in the pages of the *Enterprise*, printing a piece with a blaring, front-page headline that said: "OUR FEMALE SLANDERER. MRS. FRANK LESLIE'S BOOK SCANDALIZING THE FAMILIES OF VIRGINIA CITY—THE HISTORY OF THE AUTHORESS—A LIFE DRAMA OF CRIME AND LICENTIOUSNESS—STARTLING DEVELOPMENTS." He also published a twenty-four-page pamphlet, *Territorial Enterprise Extra, Containing a Full Account of Frank Leslie and Wife,* which included sensational details about the couple's $15,000-trip west and their personal lives (Mrs. Leslie had left her first husband, Ephraim George Squier, who was one of Leslie's editors, to marry Frank). The episode reflected Daggett's willingness to fight back in the face of even the most formidable of opponents.

Years later, Judge Goodwin, who worked with Daggett at the *Enterprise,* described his feisty coworker like this:

> Not tall, about five feet eight inches in height, swarthy, a remote strain of Iroquois in his veins, I think; heavy set, weighing close upon 200 pounds, a face full of merriment generally, but savage as a trapped bear when he was angry, a mind filled with magnetism—his like we shall never look upon again.
>
> On the *Enterprise,* I got to know Daggett as well as any one ever did, for there are not many secrets in an editorial room between men who are in close rapport every day. Daggett at that time had been a journalist for twenty-five years, and had grown lazy intellectually, but age had not withered him nor custom staled his infinite variety or his infinite humor. He was not witty, but the drollest genius in the world, and he had a way of mixing adjectives, never heard before in conversation, and when a joke was perpetuated at his expense, he would laugh until the tears ran down his cheeks.

Daggett left the *Enterprise* later in 1878, when he was elected to represent Nevada in the US Congress. Two years earlier he had been selected as one of the Republican Party's presidential electors. After being defeated in his reelection bid in 1880, Daggett was appointed the US minister to Hawaii. Following a three-year stint there, during which time he penned a well-received book on Hawaiian folklore, he retired in San Francisco, continuing to write occasionally for local newspapers and magazines. When he died on November 12, 1901, in San Francisco, the *Carson Daily Appeal* wrote, "He was one of the most trenchant writers of the country, and some of the poems he left behind were the sweetest ever to flow from a poet's pen. He. . .leaves a memory behind that will always be fragrant with the scents of the sagebrush."

The *Enterprise* Goes Dark

The demise of the original *Enterprise* in 1893 marked the end of an era in Nevada journalism. Certainly the newspaper would come back, indeed, on multiple occasions. But with each new incarnation, it became increasingly clear that something had changed. That "lightning in a bottle" captured by the "Old *Enterprise* Gang," as Howard Taylor, a former printer at the *Enterprise* once described Goodman's staff, proved to be impossible to duplicate.

Several former *Enterprise* staff members, including Drury, McEwen, and Daggett, provided colorful remembrances to the *San Francisco Examiner* upon the paper's initial demise in 1893. Daggett offered a summary of the *Enterprise*'s unique working environment:

> There were many amusing incidents connected with journalism on the Comstock in those days. It was a tough camp and the boys were generally pretty wild fellows. I remember that Goodman and McCarthy were particularly aggressive, in fact they would fight; fight at the drop of the hat and shoot, too. This was well known to the boys and consequently there was generally a row pending. If news was a little scarce Mark Twain and Dan De Quille, with their fertile brains and active imaginations, could scare up a "story" that would raise the old Harry, they well knowing that Goodman and McCarthy would back them up.

Drury was equally nostalgic and reverential: "The *Enterprise* died with its boots on. Like a brave old sport whose luck had gone to seed, the *Enterprise* met its fate with the stolidity of a desperado. The valedictory did not contain a whine or a whimper. 'For sufficient reasons we stop,' was all the editor said."

The Sunday *Carson Daily Appeal* echoed Drury's sentiments in an editorial published on January 15, 1893: "To-day the *Territorial Enterprise* passes to the silent majority after nearly thirty-five years of hard service on behalf of Nevada. It began its publication in Genoa, moved to Carson and then followed the fortunes of silver mining to the Comstock. In the files of the *Enterprise* rests the history of the State, written by the ablest pens that ever graced the journalism of the Pacific Coast."

12

The Descendants

We hope to give the paper...a raffishness of outlook suited to the
temper of a community of 350 people which maintains 20 saloons.

~ LUCIUS BEEBE, 1952 ~

THE *TERRITORIAL ENTERPRISE,* the newspaper of Twain, De Quille,
Hart, Goodman, Daggett, Doten, Townsend, and Goodwin, had been
dormant for nearly four decades when Lucius Beebe and Charles Clegg
revived it in 1952. The two were unlikely saviors of the Comstock's most
famous publication.

Beebe was a true Boston Brahmin, born in 1902 in Wakefield, MA
(about fourteen miles north of Boston) to Junius and Eleanor Beebe. The
Beebe family, whose ancestors had immigrated to America in 1650, had
deep roots in the Boston community. Beebe's father owned several successful enterprises, including a large leather business and a trust company, and
he was also president of both the Atlantic National Bank of Boston and the
Brockton Gas Company. Beebe spent a considerable amount of his child-
hood on the one-hundred-forty-acre Beebe farm in Wakefield.

He had attended a number of eastern prep schools—having been
expelled from several, due to bad behavior—before attending Yale University, which also kicked him out. He finally graduated from Harvard
University in 1927 (but only after getting suspended for hitting another student). For a short time, he was a graduate student at Harvard, and then he
worked briefly at the *Boston Transcript* before accepting a position at *The
New York Herald Tribune* in 1929. For the next twenty-one years, he worked
at the *Herald Tribune* and became one of the most famous society columnists
in America. His weekly column, "This New York," was syndicated around
the country and dealt with the comings and goings of what he called "Café

Society," which included the five hundred most influential/celebrated/interesting people in New York—as determined by Beebe.

Since his college days, Beebe had carefully crafted a larger-than-life persona for himself. He wore fashionable evening clothes most of the time, which usually included a top hat, gloves, a topcoat with tails, and a gold-handled walking stick. He dined at the most trendy restaurants, visited the most in-vogue night spots, attended the theater and every important gala, and, in general, became the embodiment of his self-proclaimed Café Society.

"Luscious Lucius" and Charles Clegg

According to his good friend Duncan Emrich, a longtime academic and former head of the Library of Congress's folklore section, Beebe "was referred to generally as 'Mr. New York,'" an honorific that delighted him. Rival gossip columnist Walter Winchell, irritatingly enough, called him "Luscious Lucius" (Winchell may have been making a snide observation about Beebe's very open homosexuality). In addition to penning his newspaper column, Beebe prolifically wrote articles for numerous magazines, including *Gourmet, Holiday, Town & Gown, Cosmopolitan, Esquire, Collier,* and many other top periodicals of the time. He also wrote or co-wrote some forty books over his lifetime.

In 1940 Beebe met Charles Clegg, a gifted photographer who was thirteen years younger, when both were houseguests at the Washington, DC, home of socialite Evalyn Walsh McLean. The two men began a close, personal relationship and a professional partnership that would last the next quarter century. Clegg was born into an affluent Youngstown, OH, family and grew up in Rhode Island. In his twenties, he moved to New York, where he worked for a department store and studied photography. The day after the Japanese attack on Pearl Harbor, he volunteered for the US Navy Reserve, became a radio technician, and was stationed in New York; Stillwater, OK; San Francisco; and Washington, DC. Following the war, he and Beebe began to work on a photography book about railroading—the first of several they would produce together during the next two decades.

Beebe and Clegg first visited Nevada in 1940, when Beebe was invited to review the premiere of the film *Virginia City* at Piper's Opera House. They fell in love with the faded but still fascinating former mining metropolis, and they were particularly impressed with the fact that it had 360 residents and 20 saloons—or one saloon for every 18 people. Nevada author Cheryll Glotfelty has written that upon seeing Virginia City, Beebe told

Clegg, "Why the alcoholic proof here is so high, and the moral tone so low, we can be perfectly inconspicuous here." During the next decade, the two would return several times.

In 1949, having tired of the New York social scene (which Beebe had almost single-handedly created and defined) and seeing the city change dramatically in the post-war period, the two decided to relocate to Virginia City. Beebe resigned his position at the *Herald Tribune,* and the two headed west in their elegant, private railcar, which they had christened the "Gold Coast." They immediately purchased and renovated the former home of John Piper, who had built the Virginia City opera house that still bears his name.

Beebe and Clegg also soon purchased the *Virginia City News* and, upon obtaining the legal use of the *Territorial Enterprise* name, rebranded it the *Territorial Enterprise and Virginia City News.* Beebe claimed to have spent $50,000 to purchase a new printing press and other necessary accoutrements to revive the paper.

The *Enterprise* Is Reborn

On May 2, 1952, the new *Enterprise* hit the newsstands. It was an intriguing blend of the old and the new: Beebe duplicated the old *Territorial Enterprise*'s typography, and he also incorporated an ornate illustration of the nineteenth-century Comstock, along with cameo-style images of Dan De Quille and Mark Twain, on the front-page nameplate. Editorially, he adopted some of the in-your-face tone of the old-time newspaper editors, while filling the pages with news about current, local events. In a May 2, 1952, Associated Press story, Beebe said of the paper: "[It]will only be as much sophistication and good grammar as will not be offensive to the Comstock."

Within a few years, with Beebe as an indefatigable promotor of both the paper and Virginia City, the *Enterprise* became the largest-circulation weekly newspaper in the state, with most of its sales actually outside of Nevada.

A fairly typical issue of the paper, published on May 28, 1954, included a provocative, front-page headline, "Ladies Launch Hair Pulling Season in Chintzy Conflict," over a story recounting a public dispute between two local "lady decorators." Apparently the two had gotten into a row "over matching samples of a client which progressed to more heated terms and was climaxed when Miss Palmer allegedly 'unlawfully and with great force and violence' smote her colleague a swift clout with her left and the battle was joined." At the end of the story, a short bulletin in bold type stated that the two had agreed to settle the matter and that all charges had been dropped.

It's difficult to tell, so many decades later, just how much of the story was true, but the manner in which it was written definitely smacked of earlier Comstock shenanigans. Beebe's editorials, sometimes appearing on the front page, also often raised eyebrows with their tone of mock-righteous indignation—and, at times, with their air of actual indignation. One such opinion piece, which appeared in the October 1, 1954, issue, stated: "The problem confronting the community of whether or not it wants to underwrite the introduction of television by cable, insofar as it concerns private residences, is a matter for individual decision. In public places of business, saloons for instance, television can, in simple terms, destroy everything Virginia City stands for."

The piece continues by noting that people visited Virginia City to experience the authentic Old West and that "these things would vanish forever with the first television set to be installed in any public place of business. Everything that public spirited citizens have tried to preserve would simply evaporate. . .this is a safety measure on which the community's continued existence and economy may depend just as surely as it does protection from fire. Perhaps more so."

"The Wild and Wooly School"

But Beebe and Clegg's biggest fake-news contributions were their Comstock "historical" stories, some of which appeared in the *Enterprise*. Historian Ronald James has described writers like Beebe, who played fast and loose with facts, as being from the "Wild and Wooly School. . . . Beebe was a great practitioner of this cause, and refused to limit himself in any way, historical or personal."

Beebe and Clegg shared most of their tall tales in books they published about Virginia City and Nevada history. One subject that the two frequently explored was the murder of a nineteenth-century Virginia City prostitute named Julia Bulette. While the truth about Bulette's backstory—including where she was born and what kind of lifestyle she led—has long been subject to conjecture, its broad outlines were embellished by Beebe and Clegg in their own inimitable way. In a chapter titled "The Legend of the Fair But Frail," which appeared in their book *Legends of the Comstock Lode,* they described Bulette as "the Comstock's first and greatest madam." She was, in Beebe and Clegg's view, an "undoubtable Creole," who, they claimed, most likely worked the red-light district in New Orleans before heading to Virginia City.

"She lived briefly and breathlessly to find herself the toast of the richest mining community on earth, the pride of the fire companies, a humane and compassionate strumpet who was tolerated by Father Manogue, and a Nevada notable who lived and died to become one of the imperishable legends of the Comstock Lode," they wrote. They went on to assert that this saintly lady of the evening, who supposedly owned dozens of sumptuous gowns, furs, a fine horse-drawn carriage, and many jewels, allegedly lived in a splendid home known as "Julia's Palace," a salon that served as the cultural center of the community. She also, they claimed, ministered to sick and dying miners during influenza outbreaks, and she was protected by all the burly miners whenever the native Paiutes would threaten to attack Virginia City. Her funeral was said to have been the finest ever seen on the Comstock, with all the local fire companies' members, in their finest dress uniforms, marching behind her "special silver handled coffin" as it was taken from St. Mary's church to the cemetery.

While Beebe and Clegg's piece was a marvelous example of the "prostitute with a heart of gold" trope, it was, in essence, just an updated version of the kind of fake news that was more common during the era of De Quille and Twain. Historians acknowledge that Bulette most likely had a well-attended send-off, but the community's respect probably had more to do with the fact that she was apparently well liked than it did with the writers' dramatic reimagining.

What is clear is that Beebe and Clegg, and also their friend Duncan Emrich, who initially served as an editor at the newspaper, were creative with other details regarding Bulette. They claimed that Bulette, in addition to being the city's most successful madam—as evidenced by her supposed accumulation of great wealth and jewels—was a beautiful, French Creole woman of noble origins from New Orleans. Recent information suggests, however, that she was born upriver on the Mississippi (although she may have claimed to have been born in England). She apparently grew up in New Orleans, and she arrived in Virginia City sometime in 1863, becoming an independent prostitute (not affiliated with a larger brothel) and living in a small dwelling (or "crib") in Virginia City's brothel district on D Street.

Historian James has written that she "was average in most respects, but Bulette was notable for attaching herself to Engine Company Number 1, becoming an honorary member and favorite of Tom Peasley, the captain. When Peasley died in 1866 after a Carson City bar fight, she was about twenty-eight, aging for her profession, and her health was failing. Bulette was seeing a doctor regularly for treatments, and one can only imagine she was dying of tuberculosis or a venereal disease."

What we also know is that on the morning of January 20, 1867, a Chinese-American servant, who occasionally tended to Bulette's needs, discovered her dead body. One or more assailants had beaten her with a piece of firewood and had finally strangled her, and they had taken some of her clothing and jewelry. Eventually, a Frenchman named John Millian was arrested for her murder. Millian apparently could barely speak English and insisted that he was innocent of the murder, but some of Bulette's stolen items were found in his possession. Millian swore that two other men were responsible for her murder and that his only part had been in trying to sell the stolen goods. Despite his protestations, Millian was convicted and sentenced to hang.

On the date of the hanging, one of the most famous observers was none other than Mark Twain, who had returned to Virginia City to give a lecture that evening. Twain was also being paid to write regular dispatches to several eastern newspapers, including the *Chicago Republican,* during his western tour. His account of the hanging notes that Millian (dubbed "Melanie" by Twain) was the first person ever to be hanged in Virginia City, with all previous deaths due to shootings, stabbings or natural causes. This was also Twain's first time to witness a hanging, and it made an impression on him: he wrote that he never wanted to see one again.

In his dispatch, Twain called Millian a "heartless assassin" because he had allegedly "secreted himself under the house of a woman of the town who lived alone, and in the dead watches of the night, he entered her room, knocked her senseless with a billet of wood as she slept, and then strangled her with his fingers. He carried off all her money, her watches, and every article of her wearing apparel, and the next day, with quiet effrontery, put some crepe on his arm and walked in her funeral procession."

Despite the attention that the story received at the time, the tragic tale of Bulette had largely faded from memory by the mid-twentieth century, when Emrich decided to conduct taped oral-history interviews (in the Delta Saloon) with local old-timers, according to James's account. However, in the interviews, Emrich repeatedly prompted his subjects to talk about her and refused to accept their indifference regarding the subject. "Emrich worked to create his own folklore for the Comstock when he found the existing one not to his liking," James has written. "Over the next ten years, Bulette became a cornerstone of local myth."

Capitalizing on the murdered woman's newfound fame, community business leaders in the early 1950s created a fake grave site for the slain prostitute, just outside of Virginia City's extensive cemetery district, and they promoted the fictional story that she was buried outside of the cemetery because proper citizens would not allow her to be interred near "decent" folks. The legend grew so much that for many years, there was a Julia C. Bulette Red Light Museum on Virginia City's C Street, and in the 1950s, the Virginia & Truckee Railroad took advantage of her growing fame by renaming the No. 13 baggage car the *Julia Bulette*.

THE BOB RICHARDS ERA

Crafting and promoting the myth of Julia Bulette was certainly one of Beebe and Clegg's most successful efforts during their stewardship of the *Territorial Enterprise*. One of their most sustained hoaxes, however, was the creation of the Virginia City Camel Races. In 1954 Beebe hired Robert "Bob" Lewis Richards—a former Merchant Marine radio operator, sometime newspaperman, illustrator, and sign painter—to serve as managing editor of the *Enterprise*. Born in Pasadena, CA, in 1911, Richards came to Nevada in the early 1950s to work for Silver State Press, a Reno printing company.

Las Vegas journalist Ray Chesson, who worked with Richards for several years at the *Las Vegas Review-Journal* in the 1960s, described him as "a poker-thin, six-footer with a round face, a small sandy mustache, and a literary style wavering between Samuel Pepys and Lucius Beebe." Chesson said that Richards usually wore a "practiced air of mystery" and, when it suited him, was "aloof to the point of glaciation."

In 1956 Richards entered the ranks of the classic *Territorial Enterprise* purveyors of fake news when he published a small item in the *Enterprise:* the results of camel races allegedly conducted that year in Virginia City. In 1964 Richards explained the genesis of the camel-race hoax:

It all began one morning back in 1956, a morning in late July, when I was managing editor of Virginia City's *Territorial Enterprise*. The night before had been a moist one, and consequently when I came to work I was oppressed by what Mark Twain, who got his literary start on the

Enterprise, called a "quinsy of the mind," but which has since come to be known as a hangover.

I crossed the street to the Delta Saloon and ordered the necessary restorative. The bartender, Edwin Colletti, who is now Virginia City's respected Justice of the Peace, was in a sportive mood.

"Say," roared he in a jocular tone, "how are we coming with those Labor Day Camel Races?"

"I'm going to announce the committee formation this week," said I without half thinking.

And so back to the newspaper.

This was the day I had to finish page one, and there was still a small four-inch hole in the thing that, as I studied it, became larger and larger because I had nothing whatever to put in it.

Then the thought intruded. Labor Day Camel Races? Committee? After all it was a true fact of history that in the early 1860s camels were used to transport salt to Virginia City's mines from the Esmeralda salt flats. . .so that was the thing done. I filled that space with the announcement that upon the upcoming Labor Day there would be a camel race in Virginia City and went on to name innocent friends as Camel Race Committee members.

The story had generated considerable local interest and had been picked up by other newspapers, so, as Richards explained, he had decided to "cut the comedy" and to announce that the races had been called off because one of the lady camels had been bitten by a rattlesnake and was unable to race. The following year, Richards had decided to repeat the hoax, making it an annual (non) event. He explained that by then, everyone had been in on the joke, and he had kept it going until 1960. That year, however, some-one had called his bluff. Scott Newhall, editor of the *San Francisco Chronicle,* which had dutifully shared the hoaxes each year, had called Richards and had asked whether, provided that the *Chronicle* supplied the camels, Virginia City could put on the races?

The fake races suddenly became a real event. During Labor Day week-end, a pair of camels, ridden by famed movie director John Huston—who was in northern Nevada filming *The Misfits*—and by millionaire sportsman and former horse jockey Billy Pearson, more or less raced down B Street during the actual inaugural Virginia City International Camel Races.

Huston won when Pearson's camel jumped over a car and plowed into a group of spectators. Fortunately, no one was hurt.

In addition to the fake and then not-so-fake camel races, Richards perpetrated several other hoaxes—or so he claimed in later interviews. In a 1963 *Las Vegas Review-Journal* account of a speech before the Southern Nevada Historical Society, Richards took credit for "some dazzling phonies" during his time at the *Enterprise*. For example, he said that he had once published a story stating that Stone Age artifacts had been discovered in Nevada by Jesuit priests, who had identified them as being twenty thousand years old. "Experts at the University of Nevada turned white at the news," he said. Another of his hoaxes was an account of what he called "Paiute petroglyphy items" that were actually "leavings of [tenth-century] Vikings on their way to the west coast." Once again, he said, "the men from the university came galloping up" to verify the story.

The reincarnated *Enterprise* of Beebe, Clegg, and Richards came to an end in 1960, when Beebe and Clegg sold the paper and bought a winter home in the tony community of Hillsborough, CA (their neighbors included singer Bing Crosby). Richards remained at the paper for a short time but departed after getting into a tiff with the new owner. He moved to Las Vegas and edited the *Las Vegas Review-Journal*'s Sunday magazine, *The Nevadan,* for several years. Eventually he relocated to Virginia City, worked for a Reno advertising agency for a time, and then returned to the *Enterprise,* which had been sold once again. In 1968, while working in the newspaper's composing room, he suffered a fatal heart attack.

As for Beebe and Clegg, they continued working on their railroad books and other projects. Beebe wrote a weekly column, "This Wild West," for the *San Francisco Chronicle,* as well as occasional magazine articles. On February 4, 1966, Beebe died of a heart attack just after finishing his morning Turkish steam bath. He was sixty-three years old.

Clegg, who inherited Beebe's $2 million estate and various properties, continued, until 1978, to own the Virginia City home he had shared with his deceased partner. Working with Duncan Emrich, he edited *The Lucius Beebe Reader,* a collection of Beebe's columns and other works, which they published in 1967. In 1979 Clegg committed suicide via a drug overdose. He died on the exact day that he reached Beebe's final age.

In the years following Bob Richards's death, the *Territorial Enterprise* passed through the hands of a variety of owners. In 1968 the Schafer family purchased the paper, along with the newspaper building on C Street. The newspaper shut down again in 1969, and then it was revived briefly in the 1980s (when I wrote my hoax) and has resumed publication several times since then. In the 2000s the *Enterprise* name became part of the nonprofit Territorial Enterprise Historical & Educational Foundation, which—in a twenty-first-century twist—today operates a website (www.territorial -enterprise.com) that uses the name. Every couple of years there seems to be an announcement about the newspaper being revived yet again.

In other words, to paraphrase one of the *Enterprise*'s most-famous alumni, reports of its death have been greatly exaggerated.

13

The Wine of Life

*The indifference to "news" was noble—none the less
so because it was so blissfully unconscious.*

~ ARTHUR MCEWEN, 1893 ~

D ID NEVADA'S EARLY newspaper scribes, who occasionally indulged in
hoaxes, puns, or other types of humorous flights of fancy, belong to an
actual literary school or movement? Or were they just a bunch of relatively
young, frontier-newspaper guys who liked to joke around? As members of
the small, Nevada-newspaper community, nearly all of the writers mentioned here knew—and largely respected—each other and, in many cases,
worked together, often at the *Territorial Enterprise*. It was not uncommon
for one newspaper to note the comings and goings of reporters and editors
from other publications in their own local-news columns.

It is also clear that these writers consciously or unconsciously influenced each other. Twain and De Quille, who worked at the *Enterprise* at the
same time, and who maintained a friendly competition, were well aware of
each other's work and of how readers and their peers received it. This was
also true for Townsend, who also worked at the *Enterprise* for a time, and
for Doten, who owned a rival Comstock paper. Add in the popular, free,
newspaper exchange, and it's easy to see how all of these Nevada journalists
would be quite familiar with the work of their contemporaries.

Lawrence Berkove, in writing about the Sagebrush School's impor-
tance, pointed out that these journalists "wrote more and better than has
been recognized and, in the final analysis, were worthy of the mineral that
drew them to the mountains and deserts of Nevada, achieving their own
Silver Age." He acknowledged that their use of sharp, well-crafted humor
helped define their style of writing. While nearly all of the members of the
Sagebrush School would undoubtedly laugh at being lumped into a literary

designation that sounds so academic and pretentious—it conjures up the old Groucho Marx joke about refusing to join any club that would have him as a member—Berkove was right: they are worthy of our attention.

While much of this book's focus has been on the humorous, clever, and witty works of the Sagebrush School (yes, I'll happily call it that), it also makes clear that these journalists were much more than purveyors of fake news and clever sayings. As previously noted, they were also playwrights, poets, moralists, critics, novelists, essayists, and, in some cases, successful politicians. And, for the most part, they were great journalists. They had strong and mostly well-grounded opinions and convictions. Despite a lack of formal training or, in some cases, much education, they were often contemplative and multilayered writers capable of depth and insight. Their hoaxes, puns, and homey aphorisms were often ways to subtly—and not so subtly—attack unfair laws or regulations or to strike back at corrupt corporations and public officials.

Comparable to the Hudson River School artists—who earned their designation because their aesthetic vision was drawn from a place (upstate New York)—the Sagebrush School members were molded by frontier Nevada and the mining camp culture. The wide-open landscape that seemed so full of possibility, coupled with the permissive, get-rich-quick mining camp environments, proved to be fertile ground for the Sagebrushers. They often started out as entrepreneurs, coming to Nevada to seek their fortunes in gold and silver mining, but they found, in the end, something equally valuable in the enormous power of the written word.

Journalist Arthur McEwen observed that Nevada was seminal for Mark Twain: it was the place where he "got his point of view—that shrewd, graceless, good-humored, cynical way of looking at things as they in fact are—unbullied by authority and indifferent to traditions—which has made the world laugh." This assessment could just as easily apply to most of the other members of the Sagebrush School. In addition to having talent, they were democratic in outlook and indignant about injustice, and they were also fun-loving, forgiving, and fair. Perhaps that was the magic formula that defined them, and what continues to make them worthy of our attention.

Given the many testimonials that appeared in print when the *Territorial Enterprise* first folded in 1893, it is obvious that those involved with Nevada's early newspapers were changed by their experiences. For those who lived long enough to reflect back on these formative years, fond memories remained for the rest of their lives.

In 1905 Mark Twain received an invitation to attend a pioneer reunion in Reno. At nearly seventy years old, Twain was too frail to travel there, but he wrote a letter to one of the organizers, Robert Fulton, publisher of the *Reno Evening Gazette* and president of the Nevada Historical Society. He reminisced that it seemed like only yesterday since he had embarked from the Overland Stage in front of the Ormsby House in Carson City:

> If I were a few years younger I would accept it, and promptly. I would go. I would let somebody else do the oration, but, for me, I would talk—just talk. I would renew my youth; and talk—and talk—and talk—and have the time of my life! . . . Those were the days! Those old ones. They will come no more. Youth will come no more. They were so full to the brim with the wine of life; there have been no others like them. It chokes me up to think of them. . . . Have a good time—and take an old man's blessing.

In this instance, Twain was telling the truth.

Selected Bibliography

THE FOLLOWING is a list of some of the works that have been useful in the writing of this book. This bibliography is not intended to be a comprehensive record of all of the sources I have consulted. Rather, it provides an overview of the various materials that provided direct and indirect inspiration for my work. It is intended to serve as a convenience for those wishing to pursue the study of frontier journalists and their writings.

Books

Beebe, Lucius. *Comstock Commotion: The Story of the Territorial Enterprise.* Stanford, CA: Stanford University Press, 1954.

Berkove, Lawrence I. *Dan De Quille.* Boise, ID: Boise State University Western Writers Series, No. 136, 1999.

Berkove, Lawrence I., ed. *The Sagebrush Anthology: Literature from the Silver Age of the Old West.* Columbia, MO: University of Missouri Press, 2006.

Carlson, Oliver. *The Man Who Made News: James Gordon Bennett.* New York: Duell, Sloan and Pearce, 1942.

Caron, James E. *Mark Twain: Unsanctified Newspaper Reporter.* Columbia, MO: University of Missouri Press, 2008.

Clegg, Charles, and Duncan Emrich. *The Lucius Beebe Reader.* New York: Doubleday Books, 1967.

Cummings, Ella Sterling. *The Story of the Files: A Review of Californian Writers and Literature,* facsimile of 1893 edition. San Leandro, CA: Yosemite Collections, 1982.

Davis, Sam P., ed. *The History of Nevada, vols. 1 and 2,* facsimiles of the 1913 editions. Las Vegas: Nevada Publications, 1970.

De Quille, Dan. *The Big Bonanza,* Apollo Edition. New York: Alfred A. Knopf, 1969.

Doten, Alfred. *The Journals of Alfred Doten, 1849-1903.* Edited by Walter Van Tilburg Clark. Reno, NV, and Las Vegas: University of Nevada Press, 1975.

Drury, Wells. *An Editor on the Comstock Lode.* New York: Farrar & Rinehart, 1936.

Dwyer, Richard A., and Richard E. Lingenfelter. *Dan De Quille, the Washoe Giant: A Biography and Anthology.* Reno, NV, and Las Vegas: University of Nevada Press, 1990.

————. *Lying on the Eastern Slope: James Townsend's Comic Journalism on the Mining Frontier.* Gainesville, FLA: University Press of Florida, 1984.

Emrich, Duncan, ed. *Comstock Bonanza: Rare Western Americana of Mark Twain, Bret Harte, Sam Davis, James W. Gally, Dan De Quille, Joseph T. Goodman, J. Ross Browne, Fred Hart.* New York: The Vanguard Press Inc., 1950.

Goodman, Joseph. *Heroes, Badmen, and Honest Miners: Joe Goodman's Tales of the Comstock Lode.* Reno, NV: Great Basin Press, 1977.

Goodwin, C. C. *As I Remember Them.* Salt Lake City: Salt Lake City Commercial Club, 1913.

Hart, Fred H. *The Sazerac Lying Club: A Nevada Book.* San Francisco: Henry Keller & Co., 1878.

Hoffman, Andrew. *Inventing Mark Twain.* New York: William Morrow and Co., 1997.

The Iowa Center for Textual Studies. *Early Tales & Sketches: Volume 1, 1851-1864.* Berkeley, CA, & Los Angeles: University of California Press, 1979.

Jackson, W. Turrentine. *Treasure Hill: Portrait of a Silver Mining Camp.* Reno, NV, and Las Vegas: University of Nevada Press, 2000.

James, Ronald M. *The Roar and the Silence: A History of Virginia City and the Comstock Lode.* Reno, NV, and Las Vegas: University of Nevada Press, 1998.

———. *Virginia City: Secrets of a Western Past.* Lincoln, NE: University of Nebraska Press, 2012.

James, Ronald M., and C. Elizabeth Raymond. *Comstock Women: The Making of a Mining Community.* Reno, NV, and Las Vegas: University of Nevada Press, 1998.

James, Ronald M., and Susan A. James. *A Short History of Virginia City.* Reno, NV, and Las Vegas: University of Nevada Press, 2014.

Lewis, Oscar, ed. *The Life and Times of the Virginia City Territorial Enterprise: Being Reminiscences of Five Distinguished Journalists.* Ashland, OR: Lewis Osborne, 1971.

———. *The Town That Died Laughing: The Story of Austin, Nevada, Rambunctious, Early-Day Mining Camp, and of Its Renowned Newspaper, The Reese River Reveille.* Boston & Toronto: Little, Brown and Company, 1955.

McWilliams, Cary. *Ambrose Bierce: A Biography.* New Haven, CT: Archon Books, 1967.

Makley, Michael J. *The Infamous King of the Comstock: William Sharon and the Gilded Age in the West.* Reno, NV, and Las Vegas: University of Nevada Press, 2009.

Morris, Roy Jr. *Ambrose Bierce, Alone in Bad Company.* New York: Crown Publishers, 1995.

———. *Lighting Out for the Territory: How Samuel Clemens Headed West and Became Mark Twain.* New York: Simon & Shuster, 2010.

Nissen, Axel. *Bret Harte: Prince and Pauper.* Jackson, MS: University Press of Mississippi, 2000.

Paine, Albert Bigelow. *Mark Twain, A Biography: The Personal and Literary Life of Samuel Langhorne Clemens.* New York and London: Harper & Brothers Publishers, 1912.

Scharnhorst, Gary. *The Life of Mark Twain: The Early Years, 1835-1871.* Columbia, MO: University of Missouri Press, 2018.

Scharnhorst, Gary, ed. *Mark Twain in His Own Time.* Iowa City: University of Iowa Press, 2010.

Smith, Henry Nash, ed. *Mark Twain of the Enterprise.* Berkeley, CA, and Los Angeles: University of California Press, 1957.

Stoddard, Sylvia Crowell. *Sam Knew Them When.* Reno, NV: Great Basin Press, 1996.

Taylor, Howard, and Steve Gillis. *Mark Twain & the Old Enterprise Gang: Reminiscences of Howard Taylor & Steve Gillis.* San Francisco: The Grabhorn Press, 1940.

Thompson & West's *1881 History of Nevada, with Illustrations.* Berkeley, CA: Howell-North Books, 1958.

Twain, Mark. *Mark Twain in Virginia City, Nevada.* Las Vegas: Nevada Publications, 1985.

———. *Mark Twain's Letters, Volume 1, 1853-1866.* Edited by Edgar Marquess Branch, Michael B. Frank, and Kenneth M. Sanderson. Berkeley, CA, and Los Angeles: University of California Press, 1987.

———. *Roughing It.* New York: Signet Classic, New American Library of American Literature, 1980.

———. *Sketches New and Old.* Hartford, CT, and Chicago: The American Publishing Company, 1882.

Walsh, Lynda. *Sins Against Science: The Scientific Media Hoaxes of Poe, Twain, and Others.* Albany, NY: State University of New York Press, 2006.

Weisenburger, Francis Phelps. *Idol of the West: The Fabulous Career of Rollin Mallory Daggett.* Syracuse, NY: Syracuse University Press, 1965.

Western Literature Association. *Updating the Literary West.* Fort Worth, TX: Texas Christian University Press, 1997.

Articles

Basso, Clarence D., "The Writings of Dan De Quille: A Catalog of Sources, 1860-2015," retrieved from www.academia.edu on January 22, 2022.

"Benjamin Franklin Used Fake News," *The Saturday Evening Post* (February 28, 2017), retrieved on October 12, 2020, www.saturdayeveningpost.com/2017/02/even-ben-franklin-used-fake-news/.

Berkove, Lawrence I., "Life After Twain: The Later Careers of the 'Enterprise' Staff," *Mark Twain Journal* 29, no. 1 (Spring 1991).

Chrystal, William, "The Strange Story of Edward P. Lovejoy," *Nevada Historical Society Quarterly* 37, no. 1 (Spring 1994).

Crum, Steven J., "The 'White Pine War' of 1875: A Case of White Hysteria," *Utah Historical Quarterly* 59, no. 3 (1991).

"Early Mark Twain Shown in Discovery," *The New York Times* (March 30, 1930).

Eichin, Carolyn Grattan, "From Sam Clemens to Mark Twain: Sanitizing the Western Experience," *Mark Twain Journal* 12, no. 1 (Spring 2014).

Harper's Weekly (January-June 1893), https://babel.hathitrust.org/cgi/pt?id=pst .000020243371&view=1up&seq=532&q1=connery, retrieved on November 9, 2020.

Lillard, Richard G., "Dan De Quille, Comstock Reporter and Humorist," *Pacific Historical Review* 13, no. 3 (September 1944).

Loomis, Grant, "The Tall Tales of Dan De Quille," *California Folklore Quarterly* 5, no. 1 (January 19, 1946).

Mac Donnell, Kevin, "Mark Twain at Ten Paces: Facts Versus Fictions in the Origin of 'Mark Twain' as a Nom de Plume," *Mark Twain Journal* 57, no. 1 (Spring 2019).

———, "Sam Clemens' Misunderstood Hoax," *Mark Twain Journal* 52, no. 2 (Fall 2014).

"Mark Twain's First Humor," *The New York Times* (August 20, 1911).

Scharnhorst, Gary, "On Samuel Clemens's Lost 'Josh' Letters: A Speculation and Three Documents," *Mark Twain Journal* 53, no.1 (Spring 2015).

Stewart, Robert, "Guests and Songs in Twain's 'Letter from Carson City,'" *Mark Twain Journal* 53, no. 2 (Fall 2015).

"Supplement to the Boston Independent Chronicle" (April 22, 1782), https://founders .archives.gov/documents/Franklin/01-37-02-0132, retrieved on October 7, 2020.

Young, Kevin, "Moon Shot: Race, A Hoax, and the Birth of Fake News," *The New Yorker* (October 21, 2017), https://www.newyorker.com/books/page-turner/moon -shot-race-a-hoax-and-the-birth-of-fake-news.

Zwahlen, Christine M., *Samuel L. Clemens, Journalist,* unpublished thesis, University of North Texas (August 1970), https://digital.library.unt.edu/ark:/67531/ metadc131313/?q=%20Climate%20impact%20on%20military%20operations, retrieved on October 15, 2021.

Other Sources

Archives of the *Carson Daily Appeal* (actual publication title varied through the years)
Archives of the *Golden Era*
Archives of *The New York Herald*
Archives of *The New York Sun*
Archives of the *Territorial Enterprise*

Index

About the Author

RICHARD MORENO is the former publisher of *Nevada Magazine* and the author of fifteen books, including *The Roadside History of Nevada, Nevada Myths and Mysteries, A Short History of Reno* (now in its second edition), and *A Short History of Carson City*. Moreno was presented with the Silver Pen Award from the Nevada Writers Hall of Fame in 2007.